'*Anti-Racist Practice* is an essential guide and tool for understanding basic yet often misunderstood language and concepts around racial discrimination and social action. The reader-friendly descriptions and illustrations are presented in ways that enhance comprehension, while also building trust and connection necessary for reducing roadblocks to socially conscious, equitable behaviours and organizational practices. Prolific scholar and person-centred educator, Thompson created this book and timeless resource for individuals of various levels of cultural understanding and competency.''

Dr Tashel C. Bordere, *Center for Family Policy & Research,*
University of Missouri

'Once more, Neil Thompson provides a publication that is not only informative and thought provoking, but also produced in a format that is easy to understand and engage with. He certainly achieves one of his principal aims regarding the need for solidarity in tackling racism alongside other unacceptable forms of discrimination. I have no hesitation in recommending this book as a terrific starting point, but also as a pathway to furthering knowledge on this essential topic.'

John McGowan, *General Secretary, Social Workers Union*

'In the aftermath of the terrible death of George Floyd and Black Lives Matter protests throughout the globe there has never been a better time to publish a beginner's guide to anti-racism. In this refreshing new book Neil Thompson identifies the multidimensional nature of racism and helpfully discusses the pitfalls and subtle intricacies involved in tackling it. Although aimed at beginners, its clear and readable style has much to offer more seasoned campaigners in the fight for a fairer world.''

Dr Paul Stepney, *Adjunct Professor, Tampere University, Finland*

'Neil Thompson is a world-leading author, and this wonderful and authentic book adds weight to the impact of his work. Racism is one of the greatest challenges facing contemporary society. With creative and critical intent, Neil dissects the concept of racism and powerfully illustrates its complex intersections between theory and practice and presents anti-racism as an urgent issue demanding personal and professional engagement. It will be essential reading for anyone looking to understand anti-racism and will undoubtedly be a leader in the field.'

Professor Jason Powell, *McMaster University, Canada*

'I remember first encountering Neil Thompson's work as a student. His extensive work on values reassured me early on that social work was the right profession for me. I felt inspired and pleasantly surprised that tackling discrimination and oppression was regarded as a core value. This aligned perfectly with my own values. I'm confident this book will firmly resonate with many social workers and others and will be considered as another valuable resource to educate, empower and equip people from all backgrounds in policy, practice and education for decades to come. 'One world, one race … the human race!''

Wayne Reid, *co-editor, Outlanders: Hidden Narratives from Social Workers of Colour from Black & Other Global Majority Communities*

'Neil Thompson is a highly respected, internationally recognized author, and he has now added yet another excellent volume to his completed works. This very timely book provides a very clear exploration of racism and its foundations at the personal, cultural, and structural levels. The descriptions and examples provide readers with impeccable clarity and focus about issues that accompany racist attitudes and practices. The practical suggestions for anti-racist practice and opportunity for reflection on personal attitudes are incredibly helpful. I will certainly be using this book in my university courses to help students develop a solid understanding of racism and how to counter racist practices, both in their professional careers and everyday lives.'

Professor Darcy Harris, *King's University College at Western University, London, Canada*

'History and more recent events continue to highlight how racism blights our society and reminds us of the work that remains to be carried out. In this updated edition, Neil Thompson sets out, in an accessible manner, some of the ideas and thinking that can help people struggling with the discomfort, feelings of guilt and powerlessness experienced when beginning to explore these issues. This edition provides more depth and looks at racism more broadly, exploring intersectionality and beyond racism on skin colour. More current difficult areas are touched on and readers can explore these in more depth to explore international rhetoric in terms of racism and other connected discrimination and oppression. As a white Welshman, Neil also situates this work as being everyone's responsibility, through our professional values as well as our humanity. He highlights how racism impacts the whole of society and is the daily lived reality for people of colour as well as other people oppressed through ethnicity and other characteristics. In that, this is a very useful beginner's guide that explores some of the terminology and definitions before opening out areas for further development. In his inimitable style, Neil offers clarity and simple learning points to help those looking to develop their thinking, making this a useful resource to help people on their journey to develop themselves, their practice with people using services, colleagues and the organizations they work for. As such, this book is a valuable addition to anyone on their journey to developing their anti-racist practice.'

Abyd Quinn Aziz *is a qualified social worker and Reader in Social Work, having been Programme Director of the MA Social Work at Cardiff University. He is also active in anti-racism and equality, diversity and inclusion.*

'Having taught courses in this area for over forty years, my one regret is that this book was not available for my courses. The book is distinctively sociological, theoretical and, at the same time, is the most practical approach to understanding and approaching racism. The book is comprehensive and acknowledges discrimination is far more than just racial. The exercises are excellent. Thompson develops unique concepts, provides great explanations of key ideas as well as developing theoretical and practical approaches. This book is not slanted toward a particular point of view, but offers an unbiased analysis of racism and ways to put anti-racism into practice. It is destined to become a classic in the field! It is truly a masterpiece.'

Dr Gerry R. Cox, *Professor Emeritus,*
University of Wisconsin-La Crosse

'A recent review of 12 reports tackling racism in the UK by *The Guardian* newspaper (25 May 2025) showed that of the 600 recommendations identified in these reports, only a third have been implemented. These reports, such as, the inquiry into the death of Stephen Lawrence, go back as far as 1981. The original recommendations cover areas such as education, business, health, criminal justice and community cohesion initiatives. Of those recommendations that have been implemented, *The Guardian* newspaper found that actions were often addressed in an inconsistent and limited way or they are too vague to access. In this Second Edition of *Anti-Racist Practice*, Neil Thompson not only provides a useful theoretical analysis of racism but also how racist ideology infiltrates our everyday lives. In addition, he highlights the consequences of not tackling racism on individuals, communities and society. The book draws of a range of sociological, psychological, socio-political, political and historical concepts, ideologies and theory to highlight the complicated aspects of racism. For example, it highlights current political debates on migration of people to the UK. It challenges ideologies that suggest migration will result in loss of a British way of life and identity. By highlighting what can be gained through tackling racism he shows how British society can be enriched. In this way the book provides tools for the reader to identify how they can challenge stereotypical, common-sense beliefs, and ideologies. Neil skilfully navigates the reader through a vast array of these complex debates in his no-nonsense way. He highlights the consequences of not adopting an anti-racist and anti-discriminatory stance. It is clear that as a society we still have some way to go to address racial inequalities and this book provides ways in which people can challenge mediocracy in everyday situations.'

Dr Suki Desai, *Independent Researcher*

Anti-Racist Practice

This newly expanded and updated edition of *Anti-Racism for Beginners* offers guidance for engagement with anti-racism and anti-racist practices in interdisciplinary areas, from social work, healthcare and youth and community work through to business management.

A range of frameworks, based on theoretical understanding and practical guidance, prompts critical thinking, encourages meaningful conversations and enables readers to play an active and positive part in promoting anti-racism. The concepts of intersectionality and allyship are central themes throughout the book and aid in tackling discrimination and oppression. Key points, practice examples and exercises allow for the integration of theory and practice.

An ideal resource for managers, practitioners and students in social work and social care, healthcare, probation, police work, counselling, education and related areas.

Neil Thompson is a well-known and highly respected author in social work and the human relations field more broadly. He is currently a visiting professor at The Open University and Wrexham University. His online platform, The Neil Thompson Academy, offers a range of learning opportunities, including leadership qualifications.

Practice Manuals for Busy Professionals

Managing Stress, 2nd edition
Neil Thompson

Effective Problem Solving, 2nd edition
Neil Thompson

Crisis Intervention, 3rd edition
Neil Thompson

Care of Older People: A Values Perspective, 2nd edition
Sue Thompson

Spirituality and Religion in Human Services: A Guide for Practitioners and Managers, 2nd edition
Neil Thompson

Anti-Racist Practice, 2nd edition
Neil Thompson

Anti-Racist Practice

Second Edition

Neil Thompson

With a Foreword by Professor Charlotte Williams OBE and an Afterword by Garth Dallas

Routledge
Taylor & Francis Group

LONDON AND NEW YORK

Designed cover image: Getty Images

Second edition published 2026
by Routledge
4 Park Square, Milton Park, Abingdon, Oxon, OX14 4RN

and by Routledge
605 Third Avenue, New York, NY 10158

Routledge is an imprint of the Taylor & Francis Group, an informa business

For Product Safety Concerns and Information please contact our EU representative GPSR@ taylorandfrancis.com. Taylor & Francis Verlag GmbH, Kaufingerstraße 24, 80331 München, Germany.

First edition published by Avenue Media Solutions 2021

British Library Cataloguing-in-Publication Data
A catalogue record for this book is available from the British Library

ISBN: 978-1-041-13124-3 (hbk)
ISBN: 978-1-041-13123-6 (pbk)
ISBN: 978-1-003-66814-5 (ebk)

DOI: 10.4324/9781003668145

Typeset in Times New Roman
by codeMantra

Contents

CONTENTS

CONTENTS

About the author

Dr Neil Thompson has been writing, teaching and training about anti-racism and other forms of anti-discriminatory practice for well over 30 years. He now works as an independent writer and producer of online learning resources and serves as a visiting professor at the Open University and Wrexham University. His online Academy offers Chartered Management Institute qualifications and a wide range of online courses available on a subscription basis, plus an online Centre of Excellence for leaders of all kinds.

He has over 50 books to his name and has been a speaker at conferences and seminars in the UK, Ireland, Spain, Italy, Greece, the Netherlands, the Czech Republic, Norway, Portugal, Albania, Turkey, India, Hong Kong, Canada, the United States and Australia.

He has qualifications in social work; management (MBA); training and development; and mediation and alternative dispute resolution; as well as a first-class honours degree in social sciences, a doctorate (PhD) and a higher doctorate (DLitt). He holds Chartered Manager status and is a Fellow of the Chartered Management Institute.

He is also a Fellow of the Learned Society of Wales and the Higher Education Academy and a Life Fellow of the Royal Society of Arts and the Institute of Welsh Affairs. He holds a Lifetime Achievement Award from BASW Cymru, an Ambassador Award from the Social Workers Union and the Dr Robert Fulton Award for excellence in the field of death, grief and bereavement from the Center for Death Education and Bioethics at the University of Wisconsin-La Crosse.

His online Academy, with free learning resources and his acclaimed *Manifesto for Making a Difference*, is at www.NeilThompson.info.

Acknowledgements

As always, I am enormously indebted to Dr Sue Thompson for the support she offers in so many ways. Our daughter, Anna, has also played her part and deserves credit.

I am grateful to Professor Charlotte Williams for providing the Foreword and to Garth Dallas for the Afterword, and the various people who have kindly offered helpful comments that helped to improve the final product. That includes Wayne Reid, Allison Hulmes, John McGowan, Paul Stepney, Jason Powell, Suki Desai, Tashel Bordere, Darcy Harris, Gerry Skelton and Abyd Quinn Aziz.

Thanks must also go to the people who have attended my training courses over the years, especially those who were brave and open enough to share their direct personal experiences. My understanding and my commitment to making a difference were very much enriched by that sharing.

This book is dedicated to everyone who has devoted their life and work to challenging discrimination and oppression.

Preface to the second edition

Not long after reaching the level of Professor of Applied Social Studies, I decided that, when it comes to promoting best practice, I could make more of a difference outside the academic world than in it. That led to a new chapter in my career as an independent writer, educator and adviser (28 years and counting). Tackling discrimination and oppression, including racism, has been a theme of my work both before and after leaving the academic world.

Interestingly, a comment that has been made repeatedly to me over the years has been along the lines of: 'You must be very brave focusing on these issues'. It has saddened me greatly that so many people feel the need to make such a comment. Why should promoting social justice by highlighting (and working to address) discrimination and oppression be assumed to be scary or risky?

Experience has convinced me that a big part of the answer to that question is the culture of fear that has grown up around anti-discriminatory practice in general and anti-racism in particular and the 'walking on eggshells' defensiveness that it has engendered (no doubt due partly to the heavy-handed approach of some campaigners and partly to a reluctance to recognize the reality and enormity of the stain on humanity that racism represents).

A major part of my motivation for writing this book is to play a part in dispelling the idea that it is acceptable to steer clear of promoting social justice because of the perceived risks of taking sides against racism.

I am not ashamed to be white (no one should be ashamed of who they are), but I am disgusted by what the history of colonialism and slavery tells us about humankind's potential for inhumanity and the legacy that continues to diminish and even destroy so many people's lives without any possible justification.

I do not feel I have a duty to challenge racism because I am supposed to 'carry the sins of the fathers'. I have a duty to challenge racism because I am a human being and it is the decent thing to do.

What I hope this book will do is play a part in dispelling that culture of fear and contribute to establishing the need for solidarity in tackling racism alongside other unacceptable forms of discrimination.

A version of this book was originally published as *Anti-racism for Beginners* (Avenue Media Solutions, 2021). It has been updated, extended and adapted to fit in the Routledge *Practice Manuals for Busy Professionals* series. Its basic messages and rationale remain the same, however. As its title made clear, it was originally written with beginners in mind, but the feedback I have received has consistently made it clear that people in various stages of their anti-racism journey can find it beneficial.

Foreword

In recent times we have witnessed a gradual but consistent undermining of efforts to tackle racial inequalities. There has been a sense that ground gained by activists, academics, practitioners and committed citizens in the past has now been subject to attrition and at times even subject to forthright challenge. This has occurred for a number of reasons, not least as a result of political will or more accurately political *won't*. You hear phrases like: 'we are beyond that now', 'we no longer need Equality, Diversity and Inclusion policies and practitioners'; concepts such as institutional racism are disputed by arguments that suggest inequalities evidenced for other vulnerable groups are greater than those experienced by some people of colour.

You might even have noted the ways in which anti-racism is undermined, pilloried or dubbed 'woke' or 'looney left'. This type of narrative feeds into everyday common-sense understandings, into organizational cultures and readily translates into discriminatory actions and/or into lethargy, denial or inaction. In 2020 the world witnessed the spectre of the murder of George Floyd which fuelled the global campaign *Black Lives Matter*. The campaign mobilized Black and White peoples in an alliance pushing for far-reaching change and action on racial inequality and racial injustice. There is little doubting that there remains a renewed focus on these issues, a willingness, collective and individual, to do more and to do things differently in proactive work towards racial equality. There is also a recognition of the need to listen to and engage with the voice of lived experience to taking anti-racist action forward. In this respect *Anti-Racist Practice* is a product of its moment, a response to mobilize and enable action.

But it is also very timely for another significant reason. Many professionals have had their enthusiasm and commitment hampered by confusion over terminology and over what is appropriate action and intervention. Too often they report an overriding sense of fear of doing the wrong thing. This reveals itself across a broad range of social professions: social workers, social care workers, health workers, housing workers and teachers, amongst others. Neil Thompson brings over forty years of experience in the field of equalities, drawing on his academic research, knowledge and experience as a trainer and consultant, to craft this concise interrogation of key concepts, ideas and approaches to anti-racism.

Many of us know and utilize Neil's previous works which have commanded the field for some decades and which have been driven by his dictum that '*racism undermines our common humanity, destroys dignity and impoverishes us all'.* This book, is similarly ethically driven, offering a clearly written account, grounded in theory but accessible in style. Neil's strength is that he does not simplify but clarifies, he does not skirt the complexity of particular concepts but elucidates them with strong and current examples from practice.

This comprehensive book offers a starting point for engagement with anti-racism providing a number of sensible frameworks for action that are built on reflective questioning and can be applied to a plethora of situations. Whilst you can read the book quickly, the ideas put forward will prompt deep thinking and undoubtedly lead to those critical conversations that enable learning. Even for those conversant with the field, there are many compelling insights in this text to guide action.

Professor Charlotte Williams OBE
Emeritus Professor, Bangor University

Why a manual?

The word 'manual' comes from the Latin word for hand (as in manual labour, manual dexterity and so on), so a manual is a *hand*book. By 'handbook' what I mean is a set of guidelines that can help in direct practice. It is not the sort of text you might scan through to look for a quote to include in an essay; it is a basis for practice. For students, this means that it is likely to be of more use to you on placement (or in preparing for placement) than in your academic work. For practitioners, it is likely to be of more use to you in reviewing and consolidating your practice than in pursuing any further or higher qualifications. It is about *making a difference.*

But don't confuse the idea of a handbook, in the sense that I am using it here, with a 'procedures manual' or set of instructions. The issues are far too complex for simply following instructions. Each section provides food for thought and insights from my own extensive experience plus what I have learned from decades of experience as an educator and adviser.

Imagine the manual as a senior colleague whose experience and knowledge you can draw on to help and guide you, but not simply as someone who will tell you what to do or make your decisions for you.

How do I use it?

This manual covers a lot of ground. To make the most of what it has to offer I would recommend that you read it through once to get the overview of the subject matter it addresses. You can then go back and re-read the chapters that appeal to you most – and, of course, different readers will have different interests. As you read through, whether first time or second, you are likely to find it helpful to be thinking about how what you are learning can be of help to you – about how the ideas can inform your practice; how they can help you prepare for an assignment and/or make sense of your own encounters with race and racism.

The renowned linguist and political commentator Noam Chomsky expresses a helpful view in stating that:

> reading a book doesn't just mean turning the pages. It means thinking about it, identifying parts that you want to go back to, asking how to place it in a broader context, pursuing the ideas. There's no point reading a book if you let it pass before your eyes and then forget about it ten minutes later. Reading a book is an intellectual exercise, which stimulates, thoughts, questions, imagination.
>
> (2013, p. 103)

Each chapter ends with an exercise. I am aware that some readers find these helpful to pull their thoughts together and to review what they have just read, while others get little or no benefit from them. Different people learn in different ways, so it is quite simple really: if you find them useful, use them; if you do not, then there is no problem in passing them by. However, it is important not to simply assume in advance that you will not find them helpful. Give them a try and then decide on an informed basis. Similarly, each chapter has a tip, key point and reflective moment to help you digest the information and relate it to your own circumstances.

A note on terminology

Language is an incredibly rich and sophisticated form of communication, but it also has significant limitations, especially with regard to such a complex, multifaceted and sensitive phenomenon as racism. What this means is that there is no ideal terminology to refer to groups or categories of people. Traditionally, the term black (often spelled with a capital B to show it is a political, rather than directly descriptive, term) has been used to refer to those people deemed to be prone to racism on the grounds of their skin colour, nationality or ethnicity. More recently, BAME (Black, Asian and Minority Ethnic) has become widely used, although widely criticized too. People of colour is now being increasingly used in the UK under the influence of US usage.

I shall be using both black and people of colour while acknowledging that neither is able to capture the diversity or complexity of the social relations involved. We shall return to the significance of language in Chapter 6.

Also in relation to terminology, I use the term 'human services' to refer broadly to those helping professions where success depends on relating positively, constructively and effectively with people. This includes, but is not limited to, social work and social care; nursing and other health professions; youth and community work; advice work; police, probation and youth justice work; counselling and pastoral work; early years work and play therapy; and education. I also use the term 'managers across all sectors'. A major focus of my work for some years now has been on management and leadership and this has made me realize that the challenges that face human services practitioners also broadly apply to managers in any work setting, and the knowledge base needed to address those challenges has very much in common. I specify 'across all sectors' to indicate that I am not referring just to managers in human services.

Introduction

Why this book?

When I began my career in social work, the focus was very much on the individual as a result of the strong influence of psychodynamic thinking. As someone with a strong interest in social justice (under the influence of my trade unionist uncle), I found this very frustrating and unsatisfactory.

But, within a few years, the situation had started to change. First, there was the radical social work movement, with its emphasis on class exploitation and poverty. This was followed by the influence of the Women's Movement highlighting the significance of patriarchy in people's lives and the Civil Rights Movement, with its emphasis on challenging racial discrimination. The Disabled People's Movement raised awareness of the widespread exclusion of disabled people from mainstream society and gradually awareness grew of other common forms of discrimination (on the grounds of age, sexuality, religion, language and so on).

There was a shift from one extreme of issues of social justice not featuring at all on the (psychodynamic) agenda to the other of their being a high priority and a major focus of social work policy and education. Issues associated with discrimination and the oppression that it gives rise to had at last come to the fore and were receiving the attention they deserved.

However, it was not all good news, as the shift of focus was accompanied in many ways with a strong tendency to: (i) oversimplify some very complex and sensitive issues (reductionism, to use the technical term); and (ii) adopting quite a rigid, dogmatic approach that was prone to dismissing any attempts to debate and explore the complexities as 'intellectualizing' and a distraction from the campaign of action.

These problems led to a number of false starts and unhelpful initiatives and made a significant contribution to a culture of fear that undermined people's

DOI: 10.4324/9781003668145-1

confidence in addressing the subtleties, while also serving as a block to learning. This led to many people being defensive and seeking to avoid the issues altogether. The core mistake was the flawed assumption that seeking to develop a fuller and more adequate understanding of discrimination and oppression amounted to avoiding taking affirmative steps (rather than seeing it as a wise basis for making sure such steps were well informed, helpful, productive and effective).

What seemed to have happened was that forms of practice rooted in an individualistic approach (psychodynamics) had been overtaken by a more sociopolitically oriented approach, but in many ways without the necessary broadening of the underpinning theory base.

What became very apparent to me was that what was needed was a *sociological* approach – that is, one that does justice to the complexities of power, social interactions, institutions, discourses and so on. Therefore, a major focus of my work over the years has been to reinsert the missing sociological dimension and thereby play a part in avoiding the problems associated with the earlier oversimplified approaches (Thompson, 2017a, 2018a,b,c, 2021).

The Black Lives Matter protests and the Kick It Out campaign have given anti-racism a new surge of emphasis, something I very much welcome, as I was becoming very concerned that much of the earlier impetus was being lost (no doubt in part because of the reductionism and dogmatism that deterred many people from engaging seriously with the issues). This fresh impetus convinced me that I could play a helpful role by pulling together in one short accessible, practice-focused book many of the key points and insights that need to be understood and taken on board if we are to make good progress and avoid what Penketh (2000) called 'the excesses of anti-racism'.

I am also hoping that this book will serve as a sort of gateway to the more advanced literature (see the *Guide to further learning* at the end of the book) and will encourage readers to continue learning and continue making a contribution to challenging racism wherever it arises. In addition, I hope that you will be able to recognize anti-racism not as just an issue (or set of issues) in its own right, but also as part of the broader field of values-based practice – that is, forms of professional practice and management that are ethically sound and rooted in a commitment to fairness and dignity (Thompson and Moss, 2026a).

My background in social work will no doubt come shining through at times, but what I want to emphasize is that, in a political context characterized by neoliberalism and austerity that has intensified racial and other inequalities, these are challenges that face all public services personnel – practitioners and managers alike – and not just those involved in social work and social care. In addition, there needs to be more recognition that racism is not only 'bad for business' in the wider commercial world, but also ethically unacceptable for any business venture in terms of corporate social responsibility. What this book offers, then, should be seen as applicable across the board in any setting where interacting with other people is a key part of what is required to get the work done.

Given the immense destructiveness of racism and the huge human costs of allowing it to persist in what are supposed to be civilized societies, there is an urgent need to do a much better job of making anti-racist practice a reality as part of a broader commitment to anti-discriminatory practice and thus the promotion of social justice. However small a part this manual can play in taking things forward, I believe that the effort will have been worth it if it contributes to some degree of better understanding of the complexities that allows for a wiser, more well-informed and – I hope – more effective approach.

The challenges of anti-racism apply to all situations where people are interact-ing, and so much of what this book offers will be of value and relevance to anyone who wants to play a part in tackling the evils of racism. However, I envisage that it will be of particular value and interest for members of the human services broadly defined as well as managers and leaders across all sectors – basically those of us involved in trying to make a positive difference to individuals, fami-lies, communities and workplaces.

CHAPTER 1

What is racism?

Introduction

In this first chapter we address the fundamental question of what is racism. This is a more important question to ask than it might initially seem. The aim, then, is to establish a baseline of clarity before building on that understanding in the chapters that follow.

Race

Before we tackle the question of what is racism, we need to be clear about what we mean by 'race'. This is because the way the word is used in everyday conversation can be very misleading. It is commonly, but mistakenly, assumed that humanity is made up of different biologically based racial groups. This then creates a platform for racism, in the sense that a key part of racism is the assumption that some racial groups are superior to others (which is then used to justify lesser treatment of the 'inferior' groups).

While there are biological differences across certain groups of people: (i) these do not fall into the neat categories that the common stereotype of race assumes to exist; and (ii) such differences that exist are superficial and of very limited significance, if any. An example I have often used on training courses I have run is this: as a white man, I could be standing next to two other men, one white and one black, and could well have more in common biologically – other than skin tone – with the black man than the white. As the saying goes: there is only one race, the human race (see Rutherford, 2021, for a detailed rebuttal of the claimed biological basis of racism).

DOI: 10.4324/9781003668145-2

Enter sociology

This is not to say that race is not a significant concept. This is an example of where we need to start thinking sociologically. Emile Durkheim (1858–1917) introduced the idea of a 'social fact', by which he meant things that are socially significant, even though they may not be tangible or concrete. For example, marriage is a social fact. It exists only in a social sense. While we may be able to observe a wedding, we cannot see, touch, feel, smell or taste marriage – yet it exists within society and is very significant as part of society.

This helps us to understand race as a social fact – the absence of a biological basis for race does not mean that the term, as a concept, is not very socially significant. That is, social facts are just as real as any other fact. As the sociologist W. I. Thomas famously noted over a century ago, the definition of the situation is real in its consequences (Thomas and Thomas, 1923). For example, if a certain group of people are deemed to be untrustworthy, then it is likely that they will find it difficult to win trust, even if they are actually very trustworthy. The lack of a biological basis of race does not prevent some people from treating members of minority groups as if they were inferior – false assumptions can have just as much of a detrimental impact as a true assumption. For example, the Equality Act 2010 bans discrimination on the grounds not only of sexual identity, but also of *assumed* sexual identity. So, if someone discriminates against someone they *believe* to be gay, then they are in contravention of the law, even if that individual is actually heterosexual. The harm done to the person discriminated against is likely to be just as severe as if they were actually gay.

Social constructionism is an approach to sociology that emphasizes the role of social processes and institutions in creating 'social constructs' – that is, concepts that are socially defined and come to act as social facts, thereby playing an important role in social life. The law is an example of a social construct, in the sense that the law has no basis in reality outside of society. If society did not exist, nor would the law. In this sense, social constructs are real. Try, for example, explaining to a prisoner that, because the law is a social construct, its consequences are not 'real'.

Race falls into this category. While it has no basis in biological reality, the fact that its existence is so widely taken for granted and so often used to justify discrimination does not mean that it does not exist as a *social construct* that is real in its consequences.

One clear aspect of the basis of racism, therefore, is the false assumption that certain groups or categories of people are in one or more ways inferior to others and therefore worthy of less favourable treatment. As we shall see, it can take many forms and work in various ways, but at its core is this false belief that there are a number of differences that justify unfair treatment. In technical terms, difference (which is the basis of diversity and therefore, as such, a good thing) becomes redefined as a deficit.

> **Reflective moment**
>
> Can you think of any times in your life where you have been aware that assumptions are being made that certain people are somehow less worthy than others? Why do you think this happens?

Sociology also helps us to understand that racism is not simply a matter of personal prejudice. As we shall see, the reality is much more complex than that, with racial discrimination also arising through such factors as cultural assumptions, institutionalized patterns of behaviour, the use of language and policies and procedures. The significance of this should become more apparent as we make our way through the chapters that follow.

Cultural racism

Traditionally the basis of racism has been biology (or pseudo-biology, to be more accurate). However, in today's world where processes of globalization bring people into contact with a much wider range of cultures than was previously the case, what we now see is what is often referred to as the 'new racism' in which the same false assumptions are made about inferiority, but now on the basis of a perceived *cultural* inferiority. For example, many Polish people (and others of east European origin) working in the UK have encountered racism on cultural grounds. While they may be defined as white and therefore not prone to the racist assumption that dark skin is a sign of biological inferiority, they may none the less face discrimination, exclusion, marginalization and victimization on the grounds of assumed *cultural* inferiority. Their culture has, to return once again to the technical terminology, become 'racialized'.

Sadly, this is not a new phenomenon, as there is a long history in the UK of cultural racism against such groups as the Irish and Romani and Travellers (I am old enough to remember the 'No Gypsies' signs that were quite common in their day). In addition, as a Welshman, I am very familiar with many people's assumptions of cultural inferiority (Huws, 2018). We shall return to these issues in Chapter 7.

So, while racism has its roots in pseudo-biology, we need to be careful not to fail to take notice of the cultural racism that can be equally devastating and destructive.

> **Key point**
>
> We tend to think of racism in simple black/white terms, literally, but the reality is much broader than this, with many groups or categories of people being subject to racism at certain times or in certain circumstances.

A term closely associated with race is that of ethnicity. It is an important concept that we will discuss in more detail in Chapter 8. But, for now, I simply want to make a link between cultural racism and ethnicity. The term 'ethnicism' is not one that has ever caught on, and nor is it likely to. However, the role of ethnicity is important because it is a key part of a person's identity. To demean a person's ethnicity, as cultural racism does, is to demean their identity, their spiritual sense of who they are and how they fit in to the wider world, with potentially highly adverse consequences in terms of confidence, self-esteem, self-respect and mental health and wellbeing. We should therefore not assume that cultural racism is any less significant, detrimental or obscene than forms of racism based on pseudo-biological assumptions.

Outcomes, not intentions

One of the complexities around racism that many people fail to appreciate is that the problem is not simply a matter of racist intentions. 'I didn't mean to discriminate' may be genuine and truthful when uttered, but if the outcome of what was said or done was detrimental to a minority group, then unfair discrimination has occurred and therefore needs to be addressed. There has been a lot of talk lately about unconscious bias and this would be relevant to how someone can discriminate without intending to do so – for example, by not realizing that they are basing their actions on a racist stereotype that they were exposed to as part of their upbringing (see the discussion of PCS analysis below) or by using language that they did not realize had racist connotations (such as referring to the 'P*ki' shop without realizing that this is a derogatory term).

The fact that these actions were not intended to cause offence or contribute to discrimination does not stop them from being examples of racism. That is, even though there were no discriminatory intentions, the outcomes were unfair and therefore unacceptable. This is why anti-racism in particular and anti-discriminatory practice in general involve an element of 'unlearning', of abandoning ideas that were inculcated in us through our culture as part of our upbringing.

TIP! Some people become quite defensive when they become aware of the need for 'unlearning', but this is neither necessary nor helpful. The key issue is being prepared to move forward positively.

This is not to say that it is never the case that people are deliberately intending to cause offence, to discriminate, alienate and so on for whatever reason. Sadly, there is no shortage of such behaviours and attitudes. But the point I am making here is that, for every deliberate racist act, there will be others that are not intentional, but are none the less problematic. These too need to be addressed (for example, via education and awareness-raising initiatives) in addition to the deliberate attempts to oppress. We shall return to this point in Chapter 9 when we discuss 'elegant challenging'.

Racism vs. racialism
In my training work around anti-discriminatory practice, I have found it productive to explain to participants the difference between racism and racialism. The former refers, as we have just been discussing, to situations where members of certain minority groups suffer detrimental consequences, whether or not those outcomes were intended.

The latter, by contrast, more narrowly refers to deliberate attempts to oppress members of ethnic minority groups. Examples would include the actions and attitudes of far-right groups who actively pursue racist outcomes due to an overtly racist ideology.

In my experience, this distinction is important because the majority of white people seek to distance themselves from such abhorrent beliefs and actions. They are quite right to say that they are not racialist. However, what they may not realize is that they may still be contributing to racism unintentionally in the ways we have been discussing here. A common comment from white participants on my training courses would be along the lines of: 'This is really helpful. I can see that, even though I am certainly not racialist, I may at times be racist by not being tuned in enough to the subtleties of how racism works.' And many participants of colour have been equally positive about how this distinction helps to clear up a lot of confusion and avoid unnecessary defensiveness, while still making the point that racism is racism, whether intended or not. This is one of the reasons why we need *anti*-racist practice, as saying 'I would not dream of doing anything racist' may well be true, but it is not enough on its own. As we shall see in Chapter 3, racism will happen unless we prevent it from doing so: it is the 'default setting'.

Conclusion
Racism, as we have noted, is a complex matter and we have only begun to scratch the surface in some ways. But, what is clear, I hope, is that there are dangers associated with trying to tackle such complex problems in simplistic ways that

do not do justice to the multidimensional nature of the phenomenon or the subtle intricacies involved.

You do not have to be an expert in sociological thinking to play an important role in promoting anti-racist practice, but you do need to be aware of the dangers of oversimplification that can lead (and have led at times) to counterproductive results, such as making people defensive and therefore reluctant to play their part in the struggles.

We shall continue the theme of complexity (and the need to wrestle with it to get positive results based on adequate understanding) in the following chapters, so this is not the end of our discussion of what racism is all about. It is just the first step in terms of peeling back some of the layers.

Exercise 1

Why, in your opinion, is it important to talk openly about racism and not try to brush it under the carpet?

What is anti-racism?

Introduction

The main point I want to put across in this chapter is that it is essential to look at anti-racism in broad terms, to understand and appreciate it holistically. This will involve explaining that anti-racism amounts to more than simply avoiding racism. It entails considering the need for cultural change and cultural competence; exploring the significance of social structures; and highlighting the need for an anti-oppressive alliance.

Tackling racism

Unfortunately, for some people, anti-racism is about protests they see on television and the campaigns they read about in newspapers or hear about in sports programmes on television, or cases going to court to claim compensation. But it is not necessarily something they connect with their own work or their own lives – it is something kept at a safe distance.

Many people see anti-racism in purely or largely legal terms – that is, as a matter of the implementation of anti-discrimination legislation. While the law has an important part to play in securing justice, the issues that need to be addressed go far beyond the legal system.

For some white practitioners or managers, it is something they might bear in mind if working with a black individual or family, but may not take into consideration in working with, say, Jewish people. Indeed, the tendency to omit anti-semitism from considerations of racism is a common tendency (Baddiel, 2021).

 DOI: 10.4324/9781003668145-3

For some students, it is something they need to incorporate into their essays in order not to lose marks. But, for many people of colour, it is an essential part of their lives, something they have to engage with just to keep their head above water. If we are to be serious about anti-racism, then we need to take on board just how harmful, destructive, disempowering and painful racism can be in so many circumstances.

So, what I want to emphasize here is that we need to avoid too narrow or self-serving an understanding of anti-racism. We need to see the big picture. PCS analysis, the theoretical framework and analytical tool we shall discuss in the next chapter, will help us to do this, but for now, we need to emphasize the need to consider the issues in broad terms in relation to policy, practice, theory and education, working relationships, power relations and so much more. This is, of course a long, long way away from the common simplistic notion of just avoiding a number of 'politically incorrect' terms (a point we shall return to in Chapter 7) or trying to avoid relying on racist stereotypes and prejudices, as if racism can be boiled down to a matter of 'bad attitudes'.

> Whenever you come across the concepts of racism or anti-racism, make sure that you adopt a broad, holistic picture of these phenomena. That way, you will be less likely to oversimplify some very complex issues.

Beyond non-racism

I have already mentioned the need to think in terms of *anti*-racist practice, rather than limit ourselves to *non*-racist practice. The latter would involve simply making sure that no steps are taken that could be construed as racist, whereas the former involves appreciating that:

i. We may be contributing to racism unwittingly if we are not sufficiently 'tuned in' to the subtle ways in which it works, and so we need to be prepared to think carefully about the issues involved and move beyond the common-sense understandings of these issues that usually leave much of importance out of the picture.

ii. Racism can be 'institutionalized' (in other words built in to how established processes and systems work). This second point is one that we shall return to later. For now, though, it is important to note that this requires us to think sociologically about racism and anti-racism. Yes, personal prejudice and bigotry are a significant part of the picture, but they are certainly not the whole story.

Howard (2021) helpfully clarifies the distinction between non-racism and anti-racism:

ANTI-RACIST PRACTICE

Non-racism: An acknowledgement that racism exists and that all humans have an equal right to respect and tolerance, but no action is taken to do anything about the existing inequalities within society that make equality impossible. This can be described as a benign passive stance.

Anti-racism: Moves from awareness to action. Understands that racism exists at different levels: internalised, interpersonal, structural, institutional and that action in relation to each is necessary to effect change. The most important difference between non-racism and anti-racism is action.

(p. 45)

Culture change

In the next chapter we shall be exploring the significance of culture as part of PCS analysis. This is because so much racism (and other forms of discrimination more broadly) comes from ideas, taken-for-granted assumptions and unwritten rules that are the core elements of culture.

When it comes to anti-racism, culture is significant in two different but related ways. First, it can be a matter of the assumptions that we have been exposed to as part of our upbringing, as part of our socialization into the cultural context we are operating in. Children learn the rules and boundaries of their culture so effectively that these become the norm, the background of understanding that we simply take for granted for so much of the time. Sadly, such cultures will generally include racist stereotypes and other such discriminatory assumptions. They do not necessarily make a conscious decision to adopt these ideas; rather, they simply 'absorb' them as they grow up and become fully fledged members of their culture.

Reflective moment

What stereotypes or discriminatory assumptions are you aware of from your own upbringing or the culture you are currently a member of?

Second, there is the prime importance of *organizational* culture to consider. Organizations develop their own cultures (and sometimes sets of subcultures), often described as 'the way we do things round here'. New recruits quickly become socialized into the new culture and soon begin to accept it as the norm. This can be a mixed blessing. On the one hand, cultures can give a sense of security and belonging and thereby contribute to higher levels of job satisfaction, wellbeing and productivity. However, on the other hand, they can also be implicated in discriminatory practices. For example, if it is the norm for a white-dominated team to pay little or no attention to cultural diversity, the result can be that black workers in the team are disadvantaged (and black applicants can be

12

CHAPTER 2

discouraged from applying for a job there). It can even be the case that workers, whether black or white, trying to put anti-racism on the agenda in a culture that gives no space to such concerns, can become marginalized or even stigmatized for 'rocking the boat' ('There you go with all that woke nonsense again').

What should be clear, then, is our holistic approach to anti-racism needs to go beyond looking at our own or even other people's language, attitudes and behaviour to taking on board an understanding of culture and a commitment to being prepared to change harmful aspects of the culture.

Once again, the basis of the problem can be largely unintentional, in the sense that members of a culture can unwittingly reinforce unhelpful aspects of it. As a parallel example, I know of men who would not dream of sexually harassing a colleague, but whose laddish behaviour and banter contribute to a sexually charged atmosphere that allows harassment to flourish.

There are therefore some important questions to ask (and answer) about culture in both the broad and narrower senses discussed here:

1. Are there any aspects of the culture(s) you are part of that are problematic in terms of racism or indeed any form of discrimination?
2. Are you possibly reinforcing or facilitating such aspects in any way, albeit unintentionally?
3. What can you do to address any such problems and help to create a more positive, inclusive and empowering culture?

Beyond cultural competence

The need for professional practice in the people professions to be 'ethnically sensitive' has long been recognized. This would include such issues as health and social care professionals needing to take account of people's ethnicity in terms of any particular cultural and/or religious needs they may have, any particular sensitivities that need to be taken into account (to avoid offending anyone's beliefs or worldview). This could include diet, skin care, hair care and so on – issues that, say, foster carers would need to be aware of and well informed about.

Cultural differences of this kind can be of particular importance at such times as a bereavement or other major loss where varying cultural traditions would shape what is seen as an appropriate response to such losses (Rosenblatt, 2016).

Increasingly, the term 'cultural competence' is being used to refer to the same need to be aware of, and responsive to, differing cultural needs, practices and perspectives. Developing such competence can be seen as an important step forward. However, it is not enough on its own. We could be incredibly sensitive to and supportive of people's cultural situation and still contribute (by omission or commission) to racist outcomes.

Cultural awareness and contributing to cultural change where necessary are therefore very important elements of an anti-racist approach, but they need to be part of a wider strategy, a point that we will return to in the next chapter.

Social structures

Sociology also alerts us to the importance of social structures and their pivotal role in creating and maintaining power imbalances and related inequalities. Basically, society is not a level playing field because of the existence of what are known as 'social divisions' – that is, the various ways in which society is divided up (class, race/ethnicity, gender, language group and so on). These divisions are characterized by relations of dominance/subordination. This means that the different groupings are not only separate from one another, but also stand in a set of hierarchical relationships (hence the role and significance of power).

Social structures reinforce and are reinforced by cultural assumptions and patterns of thought, language, behaviour and interactions. It is no coincidence, for example, that racist assumptions and stereotypes are to be found at a cultural level in a society where white people are over-represented in positions of power, while people of colour struggle to break through the infamous 'glass ceiling'.

The significance of social structures is illustrated by the way indigenous peoples have been treated and assigned a marginalized role within their own homelands – Native Americans and First Nations peoples in North America and Aboriginal peoples in the Antipodes, for example. Racism is not a 'local' problem – it exists across the globe, albeit in different ways in different contexts, shaped by differences in social structures and associated cultures.

An adequate understanding of racism and anti-racism therefore needs to be based on an understanding of not only personal actions and attitudes, not just the cultural assumptions that feed those actions and attitudes, but also the social structures and associated power relations that underpin all of these (hence our focus below on PCS analysis which takes account of all three elements, personal, cultural and structural). Ultimately, the eradication of racism will depend on the dismantling of such inequitable structures, but that is a long-term project. In the meantime, an authentic anti-racism means working together to do everything we can to challenge racism and work towards its eventual demise.

Key point

The importance of working together for common ends is the basis of allyship. Individuals working in isolation can achieve relatively little, but together far more can be achieved.

An anti-oppressive alliance

In 1989, a proponent of both anti-racism and anti-sexism by the name of Amina Mama argued the case for what she called an anti-oppressive alliance. This was in response to a situation in which feminists and anti-racism supporters were criticizing one another for failing to address each other's concerns. Understandably, each group had its own priorities, but what needed to develop was a more holistic perspective that incorporated both sets of concerns and other related sources of oppression. Mama's plea for an 'anti-oppressive alliance' can therefore be understood as a push to bring together different groups, each of which was challenging the discrimination that gave rise to such oppression. In this context, anti-racism needs to be viewed not in isolation, but as part of a broader moral-political movement to make society fairer, more humane and more equal.

Katoto and Mohamed (2021) capture this point well when they argue that:

> Anti-racism does not take a person-centred approach in seeing people as complex people with multi-layered and multi-dimensional experiences of oppression, power, disadvantage, and privilege. With a focus on experiences of racism, which is essential, this fails to acknowledge the intersectional experiences of people and their multiple oppressions. For example, a black person may experience racism as a form of oppression, and a woman may experience sexism as a form of oppression: therefore, a black woman experiences a multi-layered form of oppression with both racism and sexism combined, which consequently increases the negative impacts that these forms of oppression have on black women.
>
> (p. 71)

We shall return to this point in Chapter 5 when we discuss the important concept of intersectionality. When it comes to tackling discrimination and oppression, no one person and no one group can achieve success alone. We need to work together to support one another in achieving the common aim of promoting social justice for all.

Conclusion

Anti-racism is a huge topic, and so there is much more that can be said on the subject, But, my hope is that this chapter has provided at least a basis for further learning so that you will feel better equipped to not only carry on reading this book, but also to commit to making learning about anti-racism and other forms of anti-discriminatory practice a lifelong journey.

Exercise 2

Which aspects of anti-racism do you feel most comfortable with? Which do you feel least comfortable with? How can you build on the former and address the latter?

CHAPTER 3
_____

Theorizing anti-racism

Introduction

Unfortunately, many people see theory as the opposite of practice, as captured in the classic: 'I'm not interested in theory, I prefer to stick to practice' (as if theoretical insights have no role to play in the 'real world'). They fail to see theory as a fundamental basis of understanding to inform and guide safe, effective and ethically sound practice (Thompson, 2017b). The need to engage with theory applies to any complex forms of practice if it is to be well-informed and effective practice, but this especially applies to anti-racist practice due to the complexities involved and the relatively high price of getting things wrong by practising in ways that are ill-informed or lacking in understanding.

Consequently, the discussions of theoretical issues in this chapter are about theory *for* practice, not theory for its own sake or theory instead of practice.

Beyond the psychology of prejudice

There is a longstanding and extensive psychology literature about prejudice and its distorting effects. For many years, this was the mainstay of theory underpinning discrimination. However, under the influence of sociology, that approach has been criticized for failing to take account of wider social factors. This is not to say that the psychology of individual prejudice does not have a role to play but, rather, that it is not enough on its own. As our earlier discussions have shown, there is a need to take account of wider cultural and structural factors if we are to have a baseline of understanding that does justice to the complexities involved.

In addition, a narrow focus on prejudice fails to take account of the major role of institutionalized discrimination, nor does it explain how discrimination

                                                   DOI: 10.4324/9781003668145-4

can arise unintentionally – for example, by failing to consider the discrimina-tory use of certain forms of language (where the discrimination is 'built in' to the language used, rather than in the prejudiced mind of the person using the language).

These two sets of issues, institutionalized discrimination and language use are worthy of closer examination, and that is what we shall do in this chapter. First, though, I want to acknowledge that prejudiced individuals do, of course, exist and that racial prejudice is indeed a serious problem. However, this takes us into the territory of *racialism* and the role of certain individuals and groups. This is clearly a problem that needs to be addressed at various levels – moral, political, legal and educational – but we must not confuse it with the much wider problem of *racism* in which, as we have noted, discriminatory outcomes arise unintentionally much of the time. A focus on prejudice would have us miss this wider picture and its significance.

One aspect of such prejudice, though, that is worthy of further comment is the significance of how difference is perceived and acted upon. The basis of diversity as a value is that it holds difference to be a positive thing. The variety associated with diversity is put forward as an asset, something that gives a broader perspective, enriches our lives and helps us to appreciate the full range of human experiences and dimensions. As such, it is the oppo-site of unfair discrimination where difference is seen as a problem or threat, something to be wary or rejecting of or a sign of inferiority. For example, someone adopting a diversity approach attitude towards people from a dif-ferent national, cultural, ethnic, religious or linguistic group would see difference as a potential source of learning, broadening of experience and personal development and enrichment. By contrast, a person who adopts a discriminatory approach to such social differences is more likely to perceive people from different backgrounds as 'alien' – that is, a possible threat and/or a member of an inferior group (uncultured, unsophisticated, underdeveloped and so on).

However, we have to ask where these attitudes are coming from, which brings us to consideration of the cultural level – the way in which ideas, beliefs, unwrit-ten rules and taken-for-granted assumptions are shared across groups and across time (through socialization or 'cultural transmission'). For this reason we shall return later to the topic of culture and its relationship with personal factors on the one hand and structural issues on the other.

Institutionalized discrimination
This is a term that is often bandied about but rarely explained or clarified. In my experience, the result has been considerable confusion and misunderstanding. Once again, we need to draw on sociology.

In everyday usage, 'institution' is generally understood to mean an organi-zation or a building, a physical presence. However, in sociology it is used in a related, but different sense. It refers to how patterns of behaviour, processes, norms and expectations, meanings and relationships become so well established that they get taken for granted – they have been 'institutionalized' as a social fact. Earlier, I used marriage as an example of a social fact. It is also an institution in this sociological sense, in so far as it involves patterns of behaviour and expectations that have evolved culturally over time and, as such, are very powerful in influencing thoughts, feelings and actions.

So, when we say that discrimination is institutionalized, what we are saying is that it is not simply a matter of one or more individuals behaving in a prejudiced way. It is more a case of unfair or exclusionary patterns that have evolved over time. Examples would include:

- The lack of diversity in a university department's teaching team means that black students lack a role model who 'looks like me'.
- A recruitment process in an organization with a predominantly white workforce that relies on word of mouth to publicize vacancies systematically (albeit not intentionally) excludes black applicants, as members of local black communities never get to hear about the job opportunities.
- Black children are taught 'white' history, with significant aspects of black history not featuring or featuring in very limited ways (Olusoga, 2016).
- The alienation involved in experiencing racism is not always taken into account, resulting in an inadequate level of understanding of people of colour who are experiencing mental health problems (Fernando, 2018; Thompson, 2019).
- Services are provided in English only, placing speakers of minority languages at a disadvantage (for example, someone receiving bereavement counselling through their second language in which they struggle to express emotional nuances that they could more easily make clear through their first language).
- A training course on anti-racism focuses exclusively on black people's experiences of racism, leaving Jews, Chinese people, Irish people, Romani and Travellers and others feeling disenfranchised.

This takes us back to the point that so much of racial discrimination is unintentional, but, as I emphasized, the lack of intention does not make the unfair outcomes acceptable. The issues still need to be addressed, regardless of whether intentions were involved. Once again, we need to think more holistically about racism in particular and discrimination in general.

TIP! Remember to bear in mind that the term 'institutionalized discrimination' includes discrimination by organizations but is not limited to that. It is about established patterns that have become institutionalized or 'bedded in' to the extent that people largely do not notice they are there.

The significance of language

I developed an interest in language and languages at an early age, no doubt in large part due to being born and brought up in Wales where the Welsh language has been a prominent feature of my life. As I became interested in social justice, I started to make connections between language and inequality in two ways.

First, I was aware that the Welsh language (along with other minority languages) was consistently and repeatedly assigned second-class status, stigmatized and dismissed as irrelevant – despite the central role of language in identity formation (Griffiths, 2021).

Second, I became aware of how various forms of language could express, reinforce and mask discrimination. Initially, it was how language is implicated in sexism that I became aware of (he/man forms of language that exclude women). But, before long, I came to realize that language plays a part in other forms of discrimination too. I recognized that some forms of language that superficially seem unproblematic are actually, on more careful consideration, quite discriminatory. I began, for example, to appreciate that describing somebody as a 'third-generation immigrant' is actually quite racist. Someone who is born in a particular country cannot be an immigrant to it, and so assigning 'immigrant' status implies less than full citizenship, less than full connection with the country of their birth.

I was pleased when growing awareness of discrimination and oppression began to include consideration of the role of language. However, I was horrified when this so quickly became oversimplified by being reduced to a 'political correctness' process of banning certain words, generally without any explanation or justification for doing so (Thompson, 2018b). Such an approach fails to appreciate the subtleties involved and can also deter people from exploring further the important issues involved.

Yes, we certainly do need to pay attention to the role of language in relation to racism, but doing so in a simplistic way that assumes that the problem is just the use of certain 'non-PC' terms is woefully inadequate. A more sophisticated understanding of the role of language is called for if we are not to confuse people and dissuade them from developing a greater sensitivity to how language can express, reinforce and mask discrimination.

Unfortunately, the complex and sensitive issues relating to the relationship between language use and discrimination have tended to be oversimplified and, as such, have created a lot of problems, with many people rejecting important points about discriminatory language being dismissed as 'PC nonsense' or as 'woke'. The reality is that discrimination is often encapsulated in interpersonal interactions and, for the most part, those interactions will take place through the medium of language. Language use can therefore play a significant part in how discrimination arises and – importantly – how it can be challenged. This is such an important topic that a whole chapter is dedicated to exploring its implications (Chapter 6).

PCS analysis

I have already made the point that a focus on the individual leaves out of the picture important sociological considerations, such as cultural and structural factors. What I want to do now is to present a theoretical framework that I have developed that encapsulates all three elements, the personal, the cultural and the structural (hence PCS analysis for short).

Underpinning the framework is the idea of 'embedding'. The personal level of beliefs, values, actions and attitudes (P) does not spring from nowhere. It is to a large extent a reflection of the cultural level (C), based on a mixture of influences absorbed while growing up (socialization) and the individual's current cultural context (the power of the media to shape opinion, for example). In this sense, the P level is 'embedded' within the C level. For example, my personal views (P) have not appeared from nowhere; they are a reflection of my experience to date and that experience will have been viewed through the lens of my cultural upbringing and current cultural context (C).

But we also need to recognize that the cultural level does not exist in a vacuum. It, in turn, is embedded in the structural level, in the sense that it is no coincidence that racist assumptions, stereotypes and discourses at the C level are so common in a structural context (S) characterized by positions of power and influence being occupied predominantly by white people, so many of whom have vested interests in keeping social structures as they are. This is an example of the workings of ideology where ideas that support, reflect and reinforce existing power relations are culturally transmitted through influential social institutions, such as the media and the education system.

What is also important to emphasize is that PCS analysis is not static. To use the technical term, it is based on a 'double dialectic' (that is, two sets of mutually reinforcing interactions). This means that the Personal and Cultural levels constantly interact – cultural factors influence personal behaviour and attitudes, while personal behaviour and attitudes sustain and reinforce those cultural factors. For example, stereotypes of black people as inferior to white people feed prejudicial actions and attitudes, and those actions and attitudes will then serve to maintain the culture.

Similarly, the Cultural and the Structural levels interact. Structural factors play a major role in shaping the culture, but the culture in turn plays a part in sustaining and reinforcing those structures.

Key point

I have come across many examples (in student essays, for example) of PCS analysis being presented simply as a descriptive model. This misses the point that it is an *analytical tool*, it is an explanatory framework that can be used to make sense of complex issues by developing a picture of how personal, cultural and structural factors relate to each other.

PCS analysis is, of course, not intended as a comprehensive be-all-and-end-all approach to theory, but it does offer a useful analytical tool for helping to make sense of the complexities of racial (and other forms of) discrimination. Feedback from a wide range of people over a number of years has confirmed its value as a framework for avoiding oversimplification. It is not, of course, all that we need by way of theoretical tools to inform practice, but it does have an important role to play in making sure that we do not lose sight of the wider sociological context.

The legacy of slavery

When it comes to making sense of racism, the historic role of slavery clearly has a part to play. The idea that one person or group of persons could own another person strikes us these days as morally reprehensible and a breach of human rights. However, it was not always so, of course. From the point of view of modern sensibilities, to capture people from their homeland, remove them from their family and community and place them in forced unpaid labour appears as an act of great cruelty and inhumanity, but history shows us that there were times when such horrific injustice was considered acceptable.

Slavery in Africa existed before colonial times, dating back to before the 15th century, with rulers enslaving members of rival tribes or communities as punishment, repayment of debt or as prisoners of war. Colonialism played a key role in the development of the slave trade, with millions of people becoming victims of these inhuman practices.

Underpinning the colonialist approach to slavery was the belief that people with dark skin tones were less human than white people, if deemed to be human at all. This was the basis of white supremacy which sadly remains with us to this day in some quarters. Trading in human beings as unpaid servants was considered parallel with trading in livestock in agriculture. Its broad moral acceptance at the time is illustrated by the fact that some eminent, highly respected figures 'owned' slaves – including George Washington, Thomas Jefferson and William Gladstone.

Reflective moment

Was there anything in your upbringing that reflected – or challenged – the idea that it is legitimate to assume that white people are in some sense superior to black people?

Clearly, a key factor underpinning slavery is colonialism – that is, the practice and ideology of invading and conquering other countries to expand an empire for financial, strategic, military or gaining access to natural resources purposes.

Once again, we can see the significance of a sense of superiority, as if the colonizers have the right to subdue and exploit 'lesser' nations and communities. Griffiths (2021) illustrates this by commenting on Sir Alfred Milner who: 'in 1897 was appointed high commissioner to South Africa. Milner believed that "the British race" had a moral right to rule other people – Asians, Africans, and Afrikaners' (p. 57).

While the widespread enslavement of black people no longer applies (abolished in Britain in 1833 and the United States in 1865), the legacy of slavery is alive and well in the sense that there continues to be a strong ideological sense of colonialist hierarchy between black and white people as part of racist thinking. Sanghera (2021), in a detailed review of how imperialist thinking continues to shape modern society, states:

> The legacies of empire run deep and are sometimes contradictory. The pulling down of statues may have created the popular idea that one can erase or retain the values of empire by pulling monuments down or keeping them up, but imperialism exists within us in much more complicated ways.
>
> (p. 107)

The continuing disparity in terms of employment-based income between black and white people arising from a combination of social and political factors reflects this racial divide (Zwysen *et al.,* 2020).

But even today, slavery is not entirely a thing of the past. 'Modern slavery' involves various forms of exploitation in which individuals are controlled and treated as property, rather than as human beings. In this respect, modern slavery is parallel with historic slavery, but what is different is that the latter was based on what was regarded as legal and morally justifiable ownership of people, while the former is recognized as a crime and as morally unacceptable. None the less, modern slavery encompasses forced labour, with victims being coerced to work under threat of violence, punishment or intimidation. Human trafficking is another aspect. It entails people, through force, fraud or coercion, being exploited for sexual, forced labour or bodily organ acquisition purposes.

There is a parallel here with the distinction made earlier between biologically based racist assumptions and cultural racism, with historic slavery based on the former and modern slavery reflecting the latter.

In taking forward anti-racist initiatives, we need to get the balance right. If we focus too closely on slavery, we leave little or no room for other aspects of racism that are not related to slavery. However, if we disregard the legacy of slavery, then we fail to appreciate how significant it is – historically and currently and thereby run the risk of having a less than adequate picture of the situation that we are dealing with. A black woman participant on one of my courses made a very telling comment in this regard. She said: 'I used to feel stigmatized by having slave ancestors, but now I realize that it is the enslavers who should feel ashamed and the resilience of black people should be celebrated'.

Conclusion

It is to be hoped that this chapter has reinforced the point that anti-racism involves a set of complex issues that need to be engaged with through proper reflection and understanding. This is necessary in order to avoid the oversimplifications that have plagued many anti-racist endeavours in the past.

A sound theory base does not provide us with a set of 'answers', but it does give us a basis of understanding that we can build on over time and which can sensitize us to the subtleties that can block progress if they are ignored.

Of course, there is so much more that could be said about the theory base of anti-racism and its importance – just the origins of racism through the history of colonialism and slavery alone could easily fill a book of this size, as could an analysis of the role of capitalism or an exploration of the role of existential (in) security. But this is, after all, a practice manual, hence the *Guide to further learning* at the end of the book.

Theoretical ideas will none the less feature in the remaining chapters, not least in Chapter 8 where we examine some key terms and concepts that should help to deepen and extend our understanding. Of necessity, the range of terms to be discussed is far from comprehensive. However, it is my hope that they will be sufficient to not only clarify some key ideas but also encourage you to read and study further to extend your learning and take on board some of the more advanced concepts that can cast further light on these complex but vitally important issues.

We also need to bear in mind that, while Chapter 8 presents each term separately for ease of explanation, in reality, each of these concepts will interrelate with one or more of the others. They do not operate in isolation but, rather, as part of a complex, dynamic whole.

One very significant concept that merits a full chapter of its own is allyship, and so it is to that topic we now turn in Chapter 4.

Exercise 3

Consider an example of racism that you have come across recently (on the news, for example). See if you can apply PCS analysis to make sense of it. That is, consider what was happening at a Personal level; how did this reflect stereotypes or discriminatory assumptions at the Cultural level; and how did these cultural factors reflect the inequalities associated with social divisions at the Structural level.

CHAPTER 4

Allyship

Introduction

Some years ago, there was a saying commonly used in anti-racist circles: 'Racism is a white person's problem'. It is rarely used these days, but the wisdom behind it none the less remains just as valid today. It was not, of course, suggesting that racism is what white people experience. Rather, the point being made is that white people have some degree of responsibility for addressing racism, just as men have a responsibility to play a part in tackling sexism.

In my training courses on tackling discrimination and oppression, one of the exercises I used to use was a discussion around pitfalls to avoid. One of those pitfalls was what I referred to as 'dumping'. By this I meant the tendency to locate the responsibility for addressing discrimination with the people on the receiving end of it. It would be characterized by, for example, a man saying something like: 'I don't like the idea of my daughter growing up in a sexist society, so I hope the Women's Movement has a real impact', as if he had no role to play himself. Another example would be someone saying: 'Ageism is really unfair. I hope things have changed by the time I am old', again as if they had no part to play in bringing about change. Much the same applies to racism and anti-racism, of course.

What is needed, then, is a recognition that we all have a part to play in tackling discrimination and oppression, not just the people who are on the receiving end of any particular form of discrimination. This is where allyship comes into the picture.

DOI: 10.4324/9781003668145-5

What is allyship?

Simply put, it means being an ally to people who are experiencing and/or challenging any form of discrimination. As such, it is basically the opposite of 'dumping'. It can apply in two main ways. First, it can mean that people who are not on the receiving end of discrimination can play a part in promoting equality, diversity, inclusion and social justice in whatever reasonable ways they can.

Second, it can apply to people who are experiencing one or more forms of discrimination who can support not only people who are subject to the same form(s) of discrimination they are, but also people experiencing other forms of discrimination. For example, white women, having experienced the bitter taste of sexism, may be prepared to engage with anti-racist initiatives, and indeed other initiatives geared towards addressing discrimination and oppression.

Allyship reflects the idea that what is needed is not just *non*-discriminatory practice, but rather *anti*-discriminatory practice. For example, it is not enough for a white person to commit to not being racist or for a man to commit to not being sexist. Given the institutionalized nature of discrimination operating at cultural and structural levels, proclaiming a willingness to avoid being discriminatory at a personal level allows discrimination and oppression to go largely unchallenged at these wider, highly powerful levels.

There is a parallel here with child abuse. Refraining from abusing a child is obviously a positive thing, but clearly a teacher or other person working with children who becomes aware of abuse but fails to report it through the appropriate channels is behaving in a morally reprehensible way. In view of this, we should be able to see that being in a position to support anti-discriminatory initiatives but failing to do so is also morally questionable.

Before moving on to consider why allyship is important, we should first examine what allyship is not. I have two particular issues in mind. The first is virtue signalling. What I mean by this is the egotistical tendency to want to be perceived as doing good, of being an honourable and worthy person. Of course, there is nothing wrong with being worthy and honourable, quite the contrary, but the term virtue signalling applies as a criticism when it becomes clear that making a good impression has become the primary concern, rather than actually making a positive difference. It can be highly problematic by distracting attention from the steps that need to be taken to make a genuine difference, and it can cause ill-feeling and resentment on the part of those who suspect that virtue signalling is at the root of a particular person's behaviour. Such ill-feeling can then serve as a barrier to effective allyship.

Virtue signalling can apply in general terms where a person wants to feed their ego by being seen as someone who cares and who is 'fighting the good fight', a morally righteous person. It can also apply in a narrower sense where it relates to career progression. In organizations that value and support equality, diversity and inclusion initiatives, being seen to support them can be viewed as a potential career boost – once again, the primary focus is on making a good impression rather than necessarily making a positive difference.

TIP! Whenever you come across someone who is virtue signalling, be very careful about trusting them. It would be wiser to form your alliances with more sincere and reliable people.

It is important not to overgeneralize or be cynical here. I am certainly not suggesting that anyone who promotes anti-racism or other emancipatory initiatives is doing so just for their own benefit, but it would be naïve not to recognize that for some people at least, virtue signalling is the name of the game.

The second issue is the danger of taking over, of being a dominant presence. For example, I was once a member of a conference organizing committee developing plans to hold an event to explore anti-discriminatory practice. Unfortunately, the conference never took place. This is because, at each meeting of the committee, the attendance declined as more and more people dropped out. It was clear for all to see that the main reason for this was a white man who was very forceful in putting his own views forward and left little room for people with direct experience of discrimination to have their say. I am aware that this is not an isolated example. I suspect that in some cases it is virtue signalling once again, but at times can be a genuine attempt to help and be supportive, but one marred by a lack of self-awareness and thus insensitivity to the power dynamics being created.

This tendency to take over can apply to any form of anti-discriminatory practice, but when applied specifically to anti-racism, it is often referred to as 'white saviour syndrome'. It refers to a white person seeing their role as 'rescuing' or 'saving' people of colour from their oppressive circumstances. This appears to arise from a sense of superiority and a lack of recognition of the strengths and resilience of marginalized communities.

If we are serious about authentic allyship, then we need to make sure that we leave no space for virtue signalling or any attempts to take control.

Why is allyship important?

Being discriminated against can have profound and far-reaching consequences, and it is no exaggeration to say that it can ruin lives. Indeed, it can also end lives – for example, when the pressures involved can lead people to take their own lives; suicide at times can appear to be the only way out. In addition, racially motivated murders are clearly an extreme form of discrimination.

Racism can also shorten lives. As Sowemimo (2023) points out, racism plays a significant role in the creation and maintenance of health inequalities on racial grounds. Such inequalities have a knock-on effect in terms of life expectancy.

She describes how the legacy of colonialism and its white supremacist beliefs has created circumstances that are disadvantageous to people from ethnic minorities:

> Decolonising healthcare means radically reimagining the structure of our society. The dominant system of healthcare globally is inherently neocolonial; our understanding of health has been built on the premise that the health of some groups matters more than others and race science was established to justify the subjugation of millions of people sprawled across the European colonies.
>
> (p. 327)

She highlights how this applies also to mental health services, pointing out that young black men are ten times more likely to be diagnosed with schizophrenia than their white counterparts.

Consequently, when it comes to anti-racism, the stakes are very high, and so the positive impact allyship can make can play a valuable role in counteracting the negative outcomes associated with racism.

A further dimension to allyship relates to the generational nature of discrimination. Babies are not born with racist ideas; the development of racist views is a process of learning which involves being exposed to racist ideas embedded in the cultural level. Such cultures do not exist in any direct concrete way; as we have seen, they are social constructions. They are passed on from generation to generation through cultural transmission alongside the various other aspects of culture that play such an important role in socialization. Allyship can therefore be a key factor in trying to prevent the transmission of discriminatory ideas, assumptions and stereotypes from one generation to the next. This means that, in a spirit of allyship, parents, teachers and others who have an influence on children's ideas, beliefs and perspectives can contribute to discriminatory assumptions being challenged rather than accepted and seek to make sure that they are replaced by ideas about dignity, respect, valuing of difference, inclusion and compassion.

Allyship can also make an important contribution by helping to create and sustain a sense of solidarity. People subject to discrimination will often feel alienated and thus isolated and alone. This can be very disempowering, sapping confidence and feeding a sense of negativity and defeatism. By contrast, allyship, when it works well, can replace a sense of alienation with a sense of belonging, a feeling of solidarity that can be energizing and empowering.

Reflective moment

What experiences of isolation or alienation have you ever had? And what experiences of solidarity have you had? How can you help people avoid the former and develop the latter?

This is also important for allies who are not on the receiving end of discrimination, but who could none the less face difficulties when others mock them, try to undermine them (labelling them as 'woke', for example, as if being tuned in to discrimination is a bad thing) or otherwise present obstacles to progress. The sense of solidarity that allyship brings can be a source of confidence and sustenance in getting past such difficulties.

In effect, the basic idea behind allyship is captured by the claim attributed to the 18th-century Irish philosopher Edmund Burke that all that is necessary for the triumph of evil is for good people to do nothing. In turn, this reflects the important comment of the renowned and influential educationalist Paulo Freire (2000) that to remain neutral is to side with the oppressor.

Key point

One of the ways in which ideology works is to present the specific interests of powerful groups (the 'power elite', to use the technical term) as if they are the interests of the wider community. The myth of trickle-down economics is a good example of this. The idea is that, as the rich get richer, the benefits 'trickle down' to improve the lot of everyone, although this clearly does not happen (Monbiot and Hutchinson, 2024).

We should therefore not see allyship as one option among many, but rather as a core foundation of anti-racism and indeed of anti-discriminatory practice more broadly.

What forms can allyship take?

It can be helpful to draw on PCS analysis to answer this question and thereby highlight important steps that can be taken to promote allyship and make it a reality. As we move from P through C to S, the challenges get harder, but we should not forget that the levels are interlinked and influence each other. So, while changing our own attitudes, language and behaviour can be much easier than changing a culture or shaping the structure, each step we take at a personal level makes a positive step in the right direction.

Personal
- Be aware of racism and other forms of discrimination, whether or not they affect you directly or indirectly.
- Challenge racism whenever you encounter it. This should be done tactfully and sensitively – see the discussion below of 'elegant challenging'.

■ Seek out your organization's policy on anti-racism. This may be a standalone policy or part of a broader equality, diversity and inclusion policy or similar. Be aware of any instances of the policy not being adhered to and be prepared to raise these through appropriate channels – team meetings, for example.

■ Make it clear to colleagues that you are prepared to support them in any struggles they may encounter, but be careful not to force yourself on anyone – they may not want your support for some reason.

■ Be prepared to listen carefully and take on board what people say about their experiences of discrimination – people experience discrimination in different ways at different times, so your experience, although possibly broadly similar, may be very different from theirs.

■ Join any campaigns you may become aware of – for example, through your professional organization or trade union.

■ Play your part in making your team an inclusive, supportive, nurturing and empowering team, even if you are not a team manager.

■ If you manage staff or supervise students, be as supportive of them as you can – for example, by making it clear that they will be listened to if they have any concerns about discrimination. Offer them peer mentoring where available.

Cultural

Cultures are very powerful, but they do not have a mind of their own. They can therefore be challenged and changed in the right circumstances. Broader cultures are changing and evolving over time, so we can each do our bit to reinforce the positive elements and address the negative ones.

The same logic is applicable to workplace cultures, so this means each employee (not just those in positions of authority) can highlight and reinforce positive aspects of the culture, those that involve valuing diversity and promoting inclusion and dignity and raise concerns about any aspects that detract from social justice or fair treatment of all staff.

Cultures are based on habit which can make them very powerful and thus difficult to shift at times. However, they rely on being taken for granted and not being questioned or examined. A key role you can play, therefore, is to play your part in raising awareness of the different aspects of the culture, but doing so skilfully and sensitively so that people who feel comfortable in the culture do not feel threatened and thus become defensive (or worse, come to see you as someone who needs to be attacked). It is about consciousness raising, not about trying to impose change on people that they do not understand or do not see the need for.

When it comes to culture, it is important to get the balance right. On the one hand, we should not be defeatist about culture change by assuming that 'it's just the way things are' and there is nothing we can do about it (such defeatism actually feeds its power). But nor should we have unrealistic expectations about what can be changed or how quickly change can be brought about. It is about being cautiously optimistic and doing the best we can.

What is key to culture change is the need to work together, to strive for change through solidarity, not by acting in isolation. Indeed, this is the very essence of allyship.

Structural

Social divisions, such as class, race/ethnicity and gender are deeply entrenched in social life, and so they tend to be very difficult to shift. However, sociology teaches us that society is constantly changing and evolving, and so the opportunities to bring about positive change do exist, although the timescales are likely to be quite long. Again, it is a matter of being realistic. How sociopolitical systems operate is very complex and multidimensional, so there are no easy answers or simple solutions, but there is scope for us to play our part, individually and collectively to bringing about change over time.

If we think in terms of PCS analysis, actions at the Personal level can contribute to Culture change which in turn can play a part in gradual change at the Structural level. Consider, for example, the role of trade unions in securing better working conditions for working people and, in doing so, changing the class-based power dynamics. So, the idea that nothing can be done to change the structure of society is unnecessarily defeatist and fails to take account of the fact that society is changing all the time – the challenge is to be aware of the power dynamics and the role we can play in using collective power to bring about the changes needed to being about a fairer and more egalitarian society – however small and gradual that role may be. The task is of mammoth proportions, but we should not lose hope. As I mentioned earlier, any steps we can take in the right direction will be worth making.

Conclusion

I very much hope that the significance of allyship is now clear and that you can see the value of taking it seriously. We have explored what allyship is and why it is important and examined some important ways we can strive to make it a reality as part of promoting positive change. We have seen that at its heart is the key role of solidarity, whether that is in formal terms (for example, through professional associations or trade unions) or informally with colleagues and other potential allies in our lives.

One final important point to emphasize before we move on to Chapter 5 is that it is essential to pay attention to self-care. I have seen too many people put their own health and wellbeing at risk by allowing their admirable passion for social justice to overstretch them and create health-affecting stress. While it is vitally important that we do what we can to develop and practise allyship, we have to make sure that this is not at the expense of our own wellbeing or family relations. As Audre Lorde (1998) put it, self-preservation is a political act.

Exercise 4

What opportunities do you have to become engaged in allyship (or further engaged if you already are)? Who are the key people you could support and who are the ones that could support you?

CHAPTER 5

Intersectionality

Introduction

As we have noted, race is a socially constructed category, not a biological one. It is one of the ways in which societies divide people into categories (hence the term 'social divisions') and then attaches significance to them. That significance can be of major proportions, in many cases to the extent that it ruins people's lives. For example, the 'glass ceiling' has prevented many women from fulfilling their potential, ageism prevents a high proportion of older people from receiving the respect and dignity they are entitled to and, of course, racism has catastrophic consequences for a significant proportion of people of colour who are demeaned, excluded, alienated, bullied and generally treated as second-class citizens.

But race is not the only social category that can have such detrimental effects on people. It is just one of many. These different social divisions do not exist in isolation – they interact with one another, sometimes in obvious ways, but often in subtle not so visible ways, but playing a part in shaping an individual's lived reality in complex ways. These complex interactions can compound the deleterious effects of the inequalities and injustices involved. They can also compound the experiences of privilege – for example, while being male in a patriarchal society brings certain privileges, being white adds to that effect.

This chapter therefore explores how these dimensions of experience interact to produce a range of psychosocial dynamics, as each of these divisions connects not only with each other, but also with cultural and structural factors. These dynamics are what we call intersectionality. May (2015) makes apt comment:

> By focusing on how patterns and logics interact, and how systems of oppression interrelate, intersectionality highlights various ways in which,

 DOI: 10.4324/9781003668145-6

unwittingly, we can be engaged in upholding the very forms of coercion or domination we seek to dismantle.

(p. 5)

Dimensions of human experience

Western thought is generally characterized by an emphasis on the individual, with social factors seen largely as the background or backdrop. Known technically as atomism, this contrasts starkly with holism. A holistic approach is one that takes account of the big picture and incorporates the individual within it. Once we start looking at this bigger picture, we should be able to see that it has many dimensions.

Each of us is, of course, a unique individual, but much of that uniqueness comes from the complex interplay of those different dimensions (and how we react to them and make sense of them). Being human means being part of this complex, multidimensional network of social factors. But this is not a static picture – these various aspects influence each other, sometimes in complementary

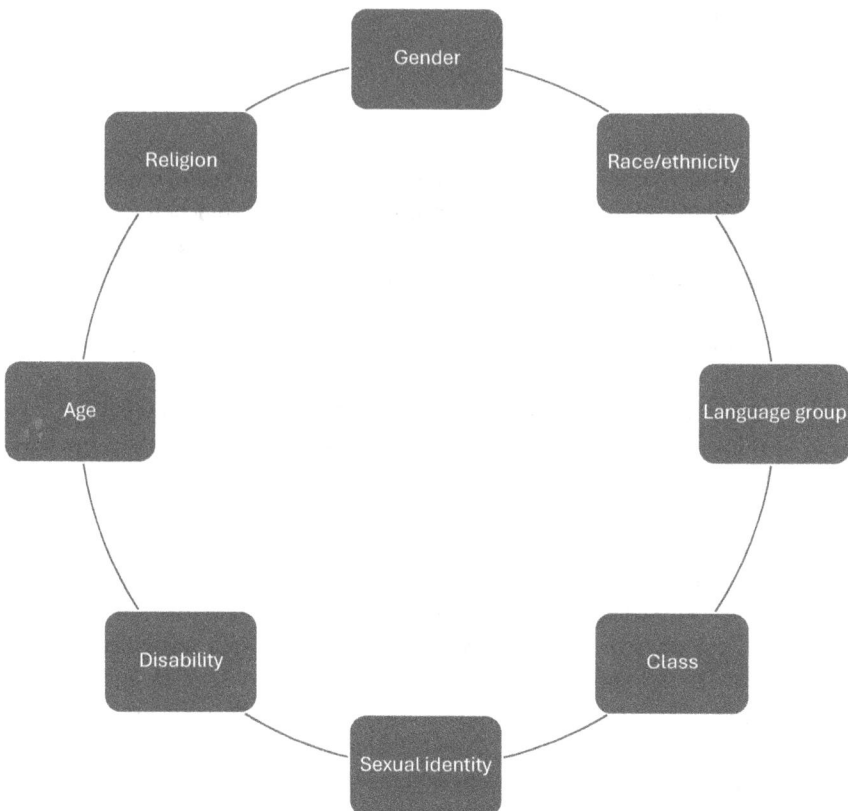

Figure 5.1 Some major dimensions of experience.

ways, sometimes conflicting. For example, as a heterosexual male, the 'messages' I receive about what it means to be a man are largely consistent with being heterosexual and therefore present me with no problems. However, if I were gay, there would be some degree of conflict between my sexual identity and the dominant messages about masculinity fed to me through the media, the education system and so on, in all likelihood in detriment to my wellbeing and possibly even to my mental health.

If we consider just how many of these social divisions or 'dimensions of experience' there are, we start to appreciate what an amazingly complex picture being human amounts to. When we also consider that this is a dynamic situation – that is, one that is constantly changing and evolving – the complexity becomes mind boggling.

If we seek to understand racism, then we need to locate it within this wider context of the constant interplay of social divisions as dimensions of experience. One way of putting this is to say that racism is not simply a form of prejudice, it is a social system that operates alongside and in conjunction with other social systems as part of a multidimensional network of social relations in general. It is therefore important to explore in more detail this concept of system as it applies to social interactions.

Social systems

There are various kinds of system. The Earth is part of the Solar System, we travel around on road and transportation systems, earn and spend money through financial systems and our bodies operate on the basis of biochemical systems. But our concerns here are with social systems. In my *Applied Sociology* book (Thompson, 2018a), I present the SPIDER framework of social:

Structures | Processes | Institutions | Discourses | Expectations | Relations

Each of these can be seen as a system, or part of a system in its own right, with each forming part of a wider interlocking system that forms much of the basis of social life. Like PCS analysis, it can be a useful analytical tool for gaining an overview of social systems and how they interrelate and influence one another.

A recognition of the role and power of systems was fundamental to the development of sociology as a social science discipline, as featured in the work of Durkheim (1858–1917) who is generally recognized as a key figure in the development of sociological ways of thinking. Systems can operate on a formal basis – the legal system, for example – and can therefore be quite visible in the way they work (or some aspects at least). However, they can also operate more informally and therefore invisibly to a large extent. Our earlier discussion of the role and power of culture exemplifies this – indeed, its invisibility is a major part of what gives it power: how can people challenge or counteract something if they have not noticed that it exists?

TIP! This is why it is important to be tuned in to issues of power and to be able to spot where power dynamics are taking place. In this case, ignorance is not bliss.

If we start to think of forms of discrimination not just as sets of harmful practices and attitudes, but as functioning systems, then we can start to see that they are (i) interlocking systems that influence each other; and (ii) less likely to be open to change by linear or non-systemic means.

As far as (i) is concerned, this takes us back to my earlier point about the need to think holistically, to see the big picture and how the different elements affect each other. For example, in planning a conference, it would be necessary to look at all the different aspects: venue and room allocations; parking and ease of access; catering arrangements; timings; speakers; audio-visual equipment; inclusion issues and so on. Missing out one or more of these considerations could lead to a chaotic or even disastrous event. However, it is also important to note getting one thing wrong could have a knock-on effect in relation to other aspects. If there is insufficient consideration of disability access, time could be wasted making ad hoc adjustments at the time to accommodate one or more people with disabilities. This could affect timings, with a consequent impact on the planned input of speakers and/or catering arrangements. Thinking about these various aspects in isolation is highly problematic; they need to be considered *in relation to one another* – this is the basis of holistic thinking.

In terms of (ii), an important aspect of how systems work is feedback – that is, how one aspect of a system affects another. For example, someone who does well in some way will receive praise and that praise is likely to boost their confidence and motivation so that they can continue to do well (or even do better). There are two types of feedback: positive (or amplifying) and negative (stabilizing). Positive feedback maintains the stability of the system, it serves to ensure continuity. An example of the latter would be how heating systems work. A thermostat regulates the level of heat the system puts out, increasing or decreasing the level according to the external temperature. In technical terms, the inputs and outputs of the system are kept in balance and thus stability is maintained within certain limits.

As this example shows, this can be very helpful. However, this is not always the case. There are times when such stabilizing feedback loops have the effect of 'locking people in' to their problems. For example, sexist assumptions that women are not well suited to management positions can prevent many women from gaining fair access to such posts. The resulting predominance of men in senior positions serves to reinforce the idea that the world of management is best served by men. This can undermine the confidence of many women who see the challenge of breaking through the glass ceiling as too great and are therefore discouraged from applying in the first place.

This example illustrates how this type of system operation 'locks people in' to a problem or set of problems. While I have used sexism as an example, the same principle applies to all forms of discrimination and, importantly, applies to how different forms of discrimination affect each other. For example, a black woman wanting to enter the predominantly white male world of management will face not only the gender-based glass ceiling, but also a parallel system or feedback loops based on racist assumptions or discourses. Similarly, racist assumptions may mean that people of colour are less likely to be invited to be members of prestigious clubs or institutions (as highlighted by Greg Dyke's comment in 2001 when he was Director General of the BBC that it was 'hideously white').

Positive/amplifying feedback works in a different way, although what it has in common with negative feedback is that it operates on the basis of the interaction of system inputs and outputs – that is information or actions affecting the system (inputs) and how it reacts to them (outputs). The outputs then serve as inputs in a new cycle of feedback and keep the wheels of the system turning.

How it is different is that, while negative feedback serves to regulate the system and thereby stabilize it (a state of homeostasis, to use the technical term), positive feedback produces significant change. Such changes are best understood as either vicious circles (detrimental) or virtuous ones (beneficial).

Stress provides a sad but very relevant example of a vicious circle. In an earlier work (Thompson, 2024), I provide a visual example of this, as shown here in Figure 5.2.

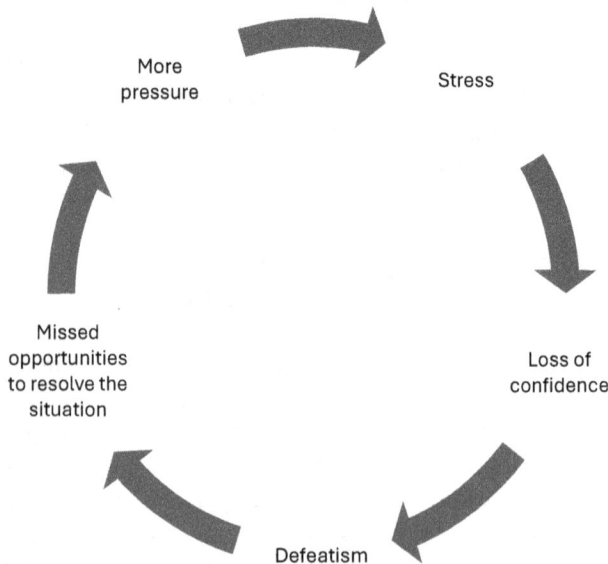

Figure 5.2 Stress as a vicious circle.

An example of a virtuous circle would be effective leadership. Consider this scenario:

> Rana has been working in a team where levels of trust and morale were rock bottom. Although she did not encounter any direct experiences of racism. no one had any faith in the manager who seemed to be uninterested in the wellbeing of team members, and so she felt uncomfortable about being the only black member of the team. However, the new team she joined was very different. The leader was very skilled in shaping a culture where people felt valued, supported and safe. This ensured a high level of morale and the leader earned a high level of trust, respect and credibility. This boosted people's confidence, motivated them to learn and be creative. Even though workload pressures were high, team members felt safe, productivity and engagement levels were high, as was the retention rate and the reputation of the team. The team was clearly going from strength and Rana felt that if any racism should arise, she would feel well supported. The manager had succeeded in creating a virtuous circle based on effective, people-centred leadership with a strong focus on inclusion.

What we should be able to see, then, is that system dynamics can work in various ways, as Figure 5.3 illustrates.

NB The way the terms 'positive' and 'negative' are used in relation to systems feedback is different from how they are used in everyday conversation:

- *Positive feedback* – everyday use: praise and affirmative evaluations; technical use: a process that amplifies (for example, a vicious or virtuous circle).
- *Negative feedback* – everyday use: criticisms and negative evaluations; technical use: a process that stabilizes (for example, family systems).

It is important not to get these mixed up.

While systems do not have a mind of their own, they do have a logic of their own – that is, they follow certain patterns, and studying these patterns is a major part of what sociology is all about. This is why it is important to: (i) examine racism holistically, so that we take account of the significant role of systems – that is, the dynamic set of interlocking relations; and (ii) understand each form of discrimination as a system, with each of those systems engaging with other systems in complex

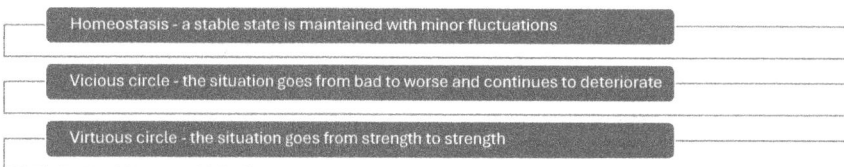

Homeostasis - a stable state is maintained with minor fluctuations

Vicious circle - the situation goes from bad to worse and continues to deteriorate

Virtuous circle - the situation goes from strength to strength

Figure 5.3 System dynamics.

dynamic ways. If we pay no attention to intersectionality, we will miss some very significant power dynamics that can have a major impact on people's lives.

Over the years I have noticed two common mistakes in relation to systems. One is the atomism I have already mentioned, which involves focusing narrowly on individual actions and attitudes and paying relatively little attention to the wider context and its systems. An example of this would be the tendency to conceive of racism primarily, if not exclusively, as a matter of personal prejudice without considering the role of cultural and structural factors and the systems they represent.

The other mistake is to go to the other end of the spectrum and regard systems as all-powerful, with little or no role attributed to human agency, thereby leaving the individual out of the picture. This approach is characterized by comments like: 'There's nothing you can do about racism, it's just the way society is'.

A useful concept here is the existentialist notion of the dialectic of subjectivity and objectivity (Sartre, 2020). 'Dialectic' refers to the interplay of conflicting forces. 'Subjectivity' refers to how we make sense of the external circumstances we find ourselves in and how we react to them. 'Objectivity' refers to those external circumstances. What this means is that, while the systems we engage with (as part of those external circumstances) have a very strong influence on us, much also depends on how we interpret and react to those influences. For example, how a particular organization operates may be based on institutionalized patterns of racism, with recruitment being based on who you know, not what you know. So, a predominantly white organization operating in this way may be systemically biased against black applicants. However, the subjective element would also come into play, in so far as different people may interpret the situation differently and/or react to it differently. The reality experienced by the people involved will therefore depend on the interaction (dialectic) of the objective and subjective elements.

Key point

It is important to avoid the mistake of focusing on either objective factors (the world out there) or subjective factors (the world as we experience it). The worlds of both theory and practice are littered with examples of how certain people have focused on one aspect to the relative neglect of the other and/or failed to take account of how each element influences the other.

In such situations, therefore, what happens is not the direct result of the system(s), but rather the outcome of the dialectical interplay of the objective circumstances (including systems factors) and the subjective reaction in terms of steps taken in response (agency, to use the technical term). This concept of the dialectic of subjectivity and objectivity is therefore helpful in avoiding the two mistakes. It is not a case of focusing on either systems or agency, but rather on both systems and agency *and* the ongoing dynamic interplay between the two.

What this means from a practice point of view is that we need to think holistically, to see the big picture, but not lose sight of the person within that picture. This needs to be a basis for our critically reflective practice.

What we also need to bear in mind is that intersectionality is not simply a matter of adding forms of discrimination together on the one hand or adding forms of privilege together on the other. We commonly get complex intersections of both discrimination and privilege. Consider the following combinations:

- Roy is privileged because he is white, male and heterosexual, but he has faced disadvantages because of his class background, regional accent and status as a minority language speaker.
- Susheela is disadvantaged by being a woman of colour, but gains privilege from being heterosexual, cisgender and the chief executive officer of the company she works at.
- Liam has suffered discrimination on sectarian grounds and as a gay man, but his extensive sporting achievements have gained him considerable respect and standing.
- Charles has a number of privileges as a powerful church elder, but this does not make him entirely immune to the detrimental effects of ageism.
- Sam is a black trans woman who has faced major challenges in her private life, but as a highly respected professor at a prestigious university, she also experiences a number of privileges.

These different combinations will, of course, produce a range of differing and unique experiences and will also vary over time. For example, while Sam is the keynote speaker at an international academic conference, her privileges will be very much to the fore, but when a few days later she visits her local pub to celebrate, she may face hostility and even aggression on the part of bigoted members of the community.

We therefore need to avoid trying to come up with some sort of simplistic scorecard of pluses and minuses, debits and credits and, instead, recognize the uniqueness of very human being and the variability of social circumstances. As with so many aspects of discrimination and oppression, the reality is very complex and does not lend itself to simple, straightforward or superficial understandings or formula solutions. Once again, we are in the territory of critically reflective practice (Thompson and Thompson, 2023).

Why is intersectionality important?
One form of discrimination may be more important than another in a person's life. For example, a gay black man may be part of a supportive black community

that 'cushions' the impact of racism to a certain extent, but that very same supportive community may treat him unfairly, even be hostile towards him because of his sexuality. If we fail to take account of intersectionality, we may miss the significance of how different systems combine to produce unique experiences for individuals, and we may be misdirecting our efforts to be supportive or empowering.

While we can recognize that intersectionality is an important theoretical concept, we also need to take on board that it has profound and far-reaching concrete implications for practitioners and managers across a wide range of contexts and settings. By recognizing the complexity of lived experiences shaped by intersecting identities and systems of oppression, we can develop emancipatory forms of practice with more sophisticated and effective approaches to addressing the associated problems. Actions that focus solely on one dimension of experience may fail to address the specific needs of those who face multiple forms of discrimination.

Reflective moment

How do the different 'dimensions of experience' and their interactions affect you and your life? How do they affect your family or friends?

An intersectional approach enables a more holistic understanding of inequality and thereby lays the foundations for the development of strategies that take account of the interconnected and systemic nature of oppression. With this enhanced level of understanding we can be better equipped to be effective protecting, supporting and empowering the people we serve and/or manage and lead.

An intersectional approach also offers a better foundation for the sort of allyship we discussed in Chapter 4. For example, practices informed by intersectional systemic thinking can help people seeking to address one form of discrimination to recognize that there are connections with other forms of discrimination and that there is much that can be achieved by contributing to the development and maintenance of an anti-oppressive alliance.

Conclusion

The concept of intersectionality provides a helpful framework for gaining an overview of the intricate ways in which various systems of oppression intersect to shape individual experiences of both privilege and oppression. By recognizing the limitations of focusing on such systems in isolation, we are able to appreciate more fully the compound effects on individuals who are subject to multiple forms of discrimination.

As such, intersectionality is a key part of the knowledge base we need in the struggle to develop more equitable, dignity-based societies and workplaces.

Exercise 5

In what ways might failing to adopt an intersectional lens make you less effective in promoting anti-racist forms of practice and management?

CHAPTER 6

Language and communication

Introduction

The relationship between language and power is a complex one that has been extensively studied. This is partly because power is so often expressed through language, but there are many other reasons too why a study of power needs to incorporate a linguistic dimension. Similarly, when examining racism and anti-racism, the role of language needs to be part of our deliberations, hence this chapter.

We begin by reflecting on the key terms of race and racism before considering the terminology used in relation to race and ethnicity and then other important linguistic issues before finally focusing on the wider picture of communication.

Race and racism

I referred earlier to the well-established idea that 'There is only one race, the human race'. The physiological or biological differences across so-called 'races' are largely superficial, variations on a theme, rather than distinct categories. However, race is none the less an important term to examine. This is because, despite the lack of biological significance, there is, as we noted earlier, much social significance attached to the term. Malik (2008) explains this well:

> There are certainly real genetic differences between human populations and the scientific study of these differences can help to unravel the roots of disease, develop new medicines, unpick the details of deep human history; perhaps eventually even tell us something about the nature of intelligence. Such genetic differences are, however not the same as racial differences.

DOI: 10.4324/9781003668145-7

> Race provides a means of not just categorising humanity, but also of imputing meaning to those categories and of selecting certain ones, based on skin colour, appearance or descent, as being of particular importance. Racial thinking divides human beings into a small set of distinct groups, sees each group as possessing a fixed set of traits and abilities and regards the differences between these groups as the defining feature of humanity. All these beliefs run counter to scientific views of population differences.
>
> (p. 3)

So, to be entirely clear, when we talk about race as form of category, it is a *social* division that we are referring to and not a biological one.

We noted earlier that a key idea in sociology is the principle that the definition of the situation is real in-its consequences. For example, if someone glares at me and rushes towards me and I interpret the situation as one of threat, the fear I feel is real even if the 'glare' was a reflection of someone with a headache and it turns out that they were rushing past me, not towards me. If we apply that principle to race, we can see that, if certain groups of people are perceived to be from different racial groups because of the colour of their skin or some other distinguishing feature and subsequently viewed either positively or negatively based on these factors, then the consequences are real: some degree of privilege for those deemed to be in a racially superior group and considerable discrimination for those deemed to be less worthy due to the colour of their skin or other such assumed marker of significant biological or social difference.

Such 'social constructions' reflect the way in which certain entities or phenomena are created or defined by society. An example of this would be social institutions, such as marriage. If there were no society, there would be no such things as marriage; money would be another example. One of the implications of this concept is that we need to be very careful not to dismiss social phenomena. Once again, it is important to be aware that the fact that race is socially constructed does not mean it is not real or not important to consider or address. If we were to claim that race is not real, then that would imply that racism is not real, and that is clearly not the case.

When it comes to terms like race and racism, we therefore need to make sure that we do not lose sight of the fact that social constructions are real in their consequences.

Ethnicity

This is a term closely linked to race. It refers to what people identify with in terms of shared culture, heritage, language, nation and other such factors. There tends to be a degree of choice in terms of how people present themselves in terms of ethnicity – for example, people from Northern Ireland may see themselves as Irish or as British. It can therefore be quite contentious at times.

> **Reflective moment**
>
> How would you describe your own ethnic identity? What are the elements that are of most importance to you?

In relation to racism, it tends to be used to distinguish between the majority ethnic group in any given context and minority ethnic groups, the latter often being subject to racism because of the ideological tendency to associate ethnicity with race. This can manifest itself in terms of the language used. For example, people from a minority ethnic group will often be referred to as 'ethnics' or 'ethnic people', as if ethnicity applies only to minority groups. The reality, of course, is that everyone has an ethnicity, but people in a majority ethnic group can take theirs for granted because it is unlikely to form the basis of racism, whereas people from minority ethnic groups do not have that privilege and face the risk of racism as a result of their minority status. The significance of this should become more apparent in Chapter 7.

As I mentioned earlier, the term 'racism' was originally limited to discrimination on the basis of skin colour, but over time it has been expanded to include what came to be known as 'cultural racism' – that is, discrimination on the grounds of a person's ethnic or national identity. For example, the European Union, with its right for EU citizens to live or work in any of the member states, has led to considerable migration and, unfortunately, widespread discrimination for minority groups who have settled outside their homeland (we shall return to this point in Chapter 7).

Another aspect of this is discrimination against Jewish people, generally referred to as anti-semitism. It is also often described as a form of racism. There the focus is not on skin colour, but on other perceived biological differences. However, there is a strong cultural element here also, with Jewish culture so often being perceived as different from that of other cultural groups. In addition, Judaism is a religion, and so anti-semitism can be included under the heading of religious discrimination (this is discussed further in Chapter 8). Unfortunately, debates about what belongs in what category have at times distracted attention from the harm and suffering such discrimination gives rise to. It is therefore essential to ensure that disputes about categorization do not stand in the way of concerted collective efforts to address racism and associated forms of discrimination.

'Correct' language

Language is constantly evolving, and not just in terms of new words being coined and added to the dictionary each year. For example, in phrases like 'One in five people...' the verb that follows should be singular to match 'one': 'One in five people believes that...', but increasingly, in both speech and writing, it is becoming more common to use a plural verb: 'One in five people believe that…'. This is just one illustration of the various ways in which language changes over time. Indeed, a common misunderstanding of language change is that it amounts to language degradation, with natural changes being viewed as 'errors' or poor-quality speech, thereby introducing a judgemental element that fails to recognize the fluidity of language usage over time (Aitchison, 2011). For example, the word 'literally' has come to mean its opposite in informal speech in recent years. Its established meaning of 'non-figuratively' is now in the process of changing to mean 'figuratively' as a means of emphasizing a point. This can have comical consequences at times, such as the widely reported estate agent's leaflet that stated that there was 'a good school literally on the doorstep', leaving people to assume that the property must have a very large doorstep indeed. But, whether people approve of changes in language use or not, language change is natural and inevitable.

When it comes to terminology relating to race and racism, I have unfortunately come across many examples of this judgementalism being used, generally with detrimental effects (for example, encouraging defensiveness and a reluctance to address such issues for fear of being chastised for using the 'wrong' word).

This situation is complicated by three main factors: (i) what is considered 'correct' language changes over time; (ii) there is no overall consensus about language use, with different schools of thought; (iii) how effectively the issues are addressed can make a big difference and (iv) many people have never had the opportunity to learn about the significance of language, and so their language use tends to reflect the culture they were brought up in.

In terms of (i), during my career, I have seen a constant process of change: equality of opportunity -> equality of outcome -> managing diversity -> valuing diversity -> equality and diversity -> equality, diversity and inclusion and, increasingly -> diversity, equity and inclusion. All this is in addition to varying uses of anti-discriminatory practice, anti-oppressive practice, emancipatory practice and social justice. Likewise, we have had a variety of terms to refer to the people who tend to be subject to racism. For many years, 'black' (or Black with a capital B to show that it was being used metaphorically) was used generically to refer to people being discriminated against on the basis of skin colour but increasingly that is being replaced with terms like 'people of colour' or BAME (black and minority ethnic), but each of these terms has its critics, so it is fair to say that there is no ideal term and what is needed is what in my earlier work (Thompson, 2018b), I referred to as linguistic sensitivity, by which I mean the ability to see which forms of language reinforce, condone or legitimate discriminatory view, actions and attitudes and which do not.

Language is a highly complex part of social life (Avineri et al., 2019); racism and anti-racism are also highly complex social phenomena. Consequently, when we look at the relationship between these two immensely complex fields, anyone who expects a simple or formula way of handling the interactions to be adequate is clearly being naïve and unrealistic. A much more sophisticated approach is called for in terms of how language works and the evolving picture of race and racism and the wider field of discrimination and oppression. No one is expected to be an expert in linguistics, but language-related issues do need to be considered carefully and dogmatic approaches avoided.

Clearly, overtly *racialist* terms need to be challenged and rejected and, in certain circumstances deemed suitable for disciplinary or legal proceedings. However, not so clear-cut uses of language can be useful 'teaching moments', rather than a basis for criticism or attack. Consider the situation I encountered on one of my training courses when a white woman participant told me of a conversation along the following lines. It took place during an interview for a place on a degree course that the participant had applied for:

INTERVIEWER: How confident do you feel, as a white person, about studying anti-racism as part of the course?

INTERVIEWEE: I'm not sure. I don't have much experience of being with coloured people, but I am keen to learn and see what I can do.

INTERVIEWER: I'm sorry to hear you use that term [coloured]; it is not acceptable. We expect better from our students.

INTERVIEWEE: [Says nothing, feels chastised and belittled, not sure if she still wants a place on the course if this is how students are treated].

She told me that 'coloured' was the term used in her family and culture and she understood it to be a polite and respectful term (and, indeed, it was once considered to be a polite term at one time, but that was a very long time ago and language use has moved on). She felt as though she had been punished for her lack of understanding, rather than be helped to learn and appreciate why such older terms were no longer appropriate. This scenario could have been much more positive if treated as a learning opportunity, rather than a patronizing heavy-handed 'correction'. People who use language that is problematic can be helped to understand what is problematic about it and be given the opportunity to explore more positive, empowering forms of language. This will help boost their confidence and capability in terms of understanding and addressing racism, whereas the interviewer's hostile approach created an obstacle to progress (the interviewer was white, by the way). We therefore need to approach issues of language in a spirit of critically reflective practice, rather than a judgemental one.

Key point

Challenging racist language is an important part of promoting anti-racist practice, but it needs to be done sensitively and constructively. Creating ill-feeling, resentment and defensiveness by using an approach that comes across as hostile or condescending is basically counterproductive (see the discussion of 'elegant challenging' in Chapter 9).

In terms of (ii), I have been disappointed on a number of occasions to hear anti-racist colleagues arguing with each other (sometimes in heated ways) about the finer points of 'correct' terminology and losing sight of the need to work together, regardless of such minor details – allyship being sacrificed for the sake of preferred terminology. As with language issues generally, it is unhelpful to think in terms of establishing the definitive 'right answer'. Recognizing the fluidity of language is a wiser option. This enables us to think not in absolute terms of right vs. wrong, but rather empowering vs. disempowering, unproblematic vs. problematic, helpful vs. unhelpful and be prepared to explore any differences of approach openly and respectfully as a basis for allyship.

In terms of (iii), it is sadly the case that there are some people who take pleasure in making sure that they are using the latest 'in' words, but who do not necessarily have a good grasp of how language can be a help or a hindrance. This can cause ill-feeling and raise suspicions of the virtue signalling I discussed earlier. If there is a reason why language use changes, then it is wise to use the 'improved' terminology, but, as I have explained, language changes anyway, so using the latest buzzwords, just because they are the latest is not helpful.

In terms of (iv) we do seem to be doing better in terms of addressing language issues through professional education, but we still have a long way to go and, of course, there will always be a significant number of people who do not have the benefit of any sort of education and training in this area. The aims of anti-racism are therefore better served by playing an educational role (tactfully, in a non-patronizing way) than by criticizing or launching an attack (see also the discussion of 'elegant challenging' below).

This theme of 'correct' language reflects two important issues. First, it highlights one of the ways in which language operates in relation to power (in terms of who is perceived to have the authority to make value judgements about other people's use of language). In general terms, it establishes a hierarchy of who speaks or writes well and whose language is deemed 'sloppy' or of lower status. Specifically in relation to racist/anti-racist language, the same issue applies, but risks serving as a barrier to allyship if power battles over the use of language are allowed to arise.

Second, it reflects an important principle, namely the dual nature of language. On the one hand, language is highly stable, and this fixity gives it considerable power. Consider, for example, the harm that can be caused by a stigmatizing label being applied to someone – such harm can persist throughout their life. It is likely that the employment chances of someone being labelled as 'mentally ill' will be considerably diminished, however unfair or invalid any such assumptions about employability might be.

On the other hand, language is quite fluid. As I have already said, it is constantly evolving. In addition, language usage will vary from context to context (in terms of (in) formality, power dynamics, social expectations and so on). Language will also vary geographically. There are not only regional dialects and articles, but also the fact that a language can be used differently in different countries. An example would be the differences in the use of English in the UK, the United States, India and elsewhere.

This dual nature of language is important because it reminds us to be cautious in addressing language issues.

Unfortunately, in the 1980s when there was a huge increase in the level of attention paid to racism and anti-racism the focus on language usage was largely unhelpful, as it was based on a grossly oversimplified understanding of the issues involved (Thompson, 2018b)

The view that there are (politically) correct forms of language that need to be used recognizes that ill-chosen forms of language can be highly problematic, but it fails to recognize the other side of the coin, the fluidity of language. Proposing that simply adopting a set of 'approved' terms is an adequate basis for addressing racist language does not do justice to the complexities involved.

Communication

So far in this chapter we have focused on the use of language, but it can be helpful to widen our focus to take account of broader issues around communication.

Communication, of course, is not merely a matter of transmitting or receiving information. It has an important role to play in shaping perceptions of race, influencing both racism itself and the potential effectiveness of anti-racist efforts.

How communication operates both reflects and perpetuates power dynamics that contribute to racial injustice. This is illustrated by the role of the media. Media discourses around race, racism and anti-racism are integral to the construction of racial identities, in so far as they shape public perceptions. They serve as a forum for the playing out of racial politics. Racial narratives are constructed and amplified through the conventional mass media (and now increasingly so in social media). For example, reporting of criminal justice issues commonly relies on narratives that present minority ethnic communities in negative terms, as alien or 'other', thereby reinforcing racist stereotypes (Rosino and Hughey, 2016).

TIP! It can be helpful to develop a sensitivity to messages conveyed through the media. If we are not alert to the nuances, we can easily be taken in.

What is also significant in terms of communication at the mass media level is the denial or playing down of racism (Dijk, 2008). West (2025) provides ample evidence of racism in modern society while also highlighting the common tendency to marginalize concerns about racism by presenting a rosy picture of race relations issues, as if to suggest that concerns about racism are overblown. This can serve to undermine anti-racist efforts and contribute to presenting supporters of anti-racism and other anti-oppressive activities as extremists, rather than as legitimate seekers of social justice and human decency towards one another. There are also opportunities for anti-racist narratives to be disseminated through the media, of course, but these will largely be crowded out by problematic representations, especially in the tabloid press.

What has been happening in the conventional media for generations is now being mirrored in digital communication in the form of social media channels. The dual nature of social media is now clearly visible, in so far as racist comments, views and images are rife, but the major platforms also offer scope for resistance, activism, support and solidarity.

A further significant aspect of communication is storytelling. Stories, whether written down or used orally, are important parts of cultural transmission, passing cultural beliefs and values from one generation to the next. Such stories can reinforce racist perspectives or serve to challenge racist tropes and assumptions. For example, the portrayal of African Americans during the Jim Crow era was based on cultural stories that reinforced racial segregation and stereotypes. These stories presented black people not only as inferior, but also as a threat to the social order (Salter and Adams, 2016). While this is a historical example, what we need to bear in mind is that, because such stories are part of cultural transmission, the underlying assumptions and perceptions can last for generations as the stories evolve and adapt to changing circumstances.

Counterbalancing this is the role of storytelling in promoting marginalized voices and highlighting the strengths and resilience of minority ethnic communities and promoting solidarity and pride (McNeil-Young *et al.*, 2023). For example, Native American tribal stories give positive messages about history, heritage, identity and worth.

Last but not least is the role of nonverbal communication (NVC). Body language works in very subtle but very powerful ways to convey messages and reactions. It can play a significant role in terms of how racism operates and how anti-racist efforts can be enhanced by the effective use of NVC. As with media-based communications, NVC is a two-edged sword. Nonverbal cues will often be used to perpetuate stereotypes, but they can also form the basis of promoting empathy and understanding across different racial/ethnic groups and thereby provide a sound foundation for anti-racist initiatives.

Forms of racial bias commonly manifest themselves through NVC. For example, expressions of disapproval or disdain can be quite overt or quite nuanced (rolling our eyes, frowning, gently shaking our head and so on). Where these are directed at people of colour, they can contribute to a sense of marginalization and alienation (Mekawi and Todd, 2021).

Once again, though, we see the dual nature of communication, in so far as NVC can be used to express solidarity and support in a spirit of empathy and allyship (Nelson *et al.*, 2011). This means that training people in the effective use of NVC can be an important foundation of anti-racist practice.

We should note, then, that NVC is not simply an accompaniment to verbal communication; it is a powerful tool that can be used to perpetuate racism or, equally to challenge racism and promote anti-racism.

Conclusion

Language and communication are clearly key elements when it comes to understanding and addressing racism and working towards racial justice. It is to be hoped that this chapter has demonstrated the need to move away from the simplistic and reductionist approach to the relationship between language and discrimination. It should also be clear that language use is only part of the much broader field of communication, and it is this broader picture that we need to take on board.

Exercise 6

Spend some time watching people use nonverbal communication. Can you identify from this what aspects of NVC you could put to good use in promoting anti-racism?

CHAPTER 7

Beyond Black and White

Introduction

The strong, longstanding and well-established link between racism and slavery has produced a situation where, for a significant proportion of people, racism relates primarily, if not exclusively, to discrimination against black people. This chapter seeks to go beyond this conception of racism to highlight a number of other forms of racially based discrimination. We shall explore in turn a number of such variations on the theme of racism, but the coverage is by no means exhaustive.

We begin with an examination of anti-semitism, a very significant form of discrimination that overlaps with religious discrimination, and so it will also feature in Chapter 8.

Anti-semitism

Of course, when anti-semitism is being considered, the Holocaust is likely to come to mind. The systematic annihilation of millions of people was and is a major stain on humanity. The fact that a political regime could not only kill so many people on the basis of assumed biological inferiority, but also do so with the support of so many ordinary people beggars belief. There are no words to capture the full horror and inhumanity of this catastrophic episode of history.

However, what we need to be aware of is that the hatred on which the Holocaust was based was not a new development at that time and nor was the revulsion at these dreadful events enough to put an end to it. Looking back historically, Hernon (2020) points out that Karl Marx and George Bernard Shaw openly expressed anti-Jewish sentiments. And, of course, Shakespeare's *Merchant of*

DOI: 10.4324/9781003668145-8

Venice is based on a stereotype of Jewish people. The same stereotypes persist to this very day (Baddiel, 2021), with this persistent discourse that presents Jews as wealthy people who pull the strings of the financial world and of society more broadly. Shabi (2024) rightly challenges this discourse. She argues that anti-semitism is basically a conspiracy theory about power. Perceiving Jews to be 'a secret shadowy elite ruling the world' (as the stereotype would have it) first of all assumes that such an overgeneralization is valid and, second, implies that any such positions of power where they may exist are unjustified and illegitimate.

Neuberger (2019) argues that not only does anti-semitism persist to the present day, but also that it is actually increasing. To say that the Israel-Palestine conflict has clearly not helped in this regard is, of course, a major understatement. She offers a helpful comment on the definition of anti-semitism:

> The Oxford English Dictionary defines antisemitism as 'hostility to or prejudice against Jews'. As a very basic definition, it is fine. But it does not help us when it comes to understanding antisemitism in all its many and varied forms.
>
> (p. 37)

This takes us back to PCS analysis and the need to look holistically at discrimination by taking account of cultural and structural factors (and how they interrelate dynamically), rather than limit our understanding to what goes on at the personal level. Once again, then, we need to be prepared to think holistically about anti-semitism as a system of oppression and not simply a matter of personal prejudice.

Hart (2021) explains why anti-semitism needs to be understood as a form of racism:

> While Judaism is a faith practised by Jewish people, there are many people who are atheist, agnostic or humanist. Being Jewish is more than the faith of Judaism and that's why we're protected from discrimination on the basis of race and ethnicity as well as religion under the Equality Act 2010.
>
> (p. 83)

Just as other forms of racism can be overt and explicit or more subtle and nuanced, anti-semitism can vary in terms of how it is manifested. At one extreme are the Holocaust deniers, those right-wing supporters who disregard all the evidence to the contrary and continue a morally repugnant tradition of demeaning Jewish people. However, it is important to be aware that anti-semitism is so woven into dominant cultural narratives that discrimination can – and does – occur without there being any specific intention or desire to undermine the rights or wellbeing of Jewish people. We therefore need to be careful not to associate anti-semitism only with its extreme version and fail to take account of its more day-to-day manifestations.

What complicates matters is that criticisms of the actions of Israel towards the Palestinian people have been deemed to be anti-semitic in some quarters. Shavit (2014) highlights the dilemma:

> On the one hand, Israel is the only nation in the West that is occupying another people. On the other hand, Israel is the only nation in the West that is existentially threatened. Both occupation and intimidation make the Israeli condition unique. Intimidation and occupation have become the two pillars of our condition.
>
> (p. xii)

He was writing this before the Russian invasion of Ukraine in 2022, but the basic point he was making remains valid. He goes on to argue that the political left has tended to emphasize the occupation element, while the political right has focused on the intimidation, neither paying significant attention to the other element or the other point of view. He concludes that: 'Any school of thought that does not relate seriously to these two fundamentals is bound to be flawed and futile' (p. xii).

Shabi (2024) adopts a similar position. She cleverly uses the term 'off-white' to characterize the dual position of Jewish people: 'White Jews aren't not white. But we aren't really *white* white either. We are off-white' (p. 10). In some ways, the majority of Jewish people are seen as white and thus part of the dominant group in power terms, but they are also subject to racism in the ways I have just outlined. The notion of being 'off-white' captures this duality and highlights some of the complexities involved.

Key point

These complexities reinforce the need to avoid oversimplifying the issues involved. Once again, what is needed is an approach based on critically reflective practice. The price to be paid for adopting a narrow simplistic approach is far too high.

Romani people and Travellers
Negative attitudes towards Romani people, gypsies and the Traveller community is so deeply ingrained at a cultural level that this form of racism is often left out of the picture altogether. Referencing the work of Loveland and Popescu (2016), Allen *et al.* (2021) make the point that:

> it's difficult to find a newspaper article, news story, television programme, film or social media post about Gypsy, Roma and Traveller people that doesn't demonise them. For us ... the demonisation of anyone, let alone

a whole community of people, seems absurd, but understanding how these stereotypes serve to sustain and justify centuries of oppression is important.

(p. 65)

This wholesale vilification of a group or community on the basis of a perceived cultural 'deficit' (not just culturally *different* from the mainstream, but perceived to be culturally *inferior*) would put this type of discrimination under the heading of the 'new' racism (as opposed to traditional racism based on biological assumptions). However, racism against Romani and Traveller people is certainly not new. It has a long, long history.

'Romani' or 'Roma' is an umbrella term that incorporates a range of ethnic groups and communities identified by their distinctive cultural, linguistic, and historical characteristics. This includes groups such as Sinti, Kale and Travellers, among others (Moreira *et al.*, 2023).

The commonly associated term of 'gypsies' is believed to be a corruption of the word 'Egyptians'. This comes from the days when Roma people who actually came from India were mistakenly assumed to be Egyptian (Cohen, 2024). The term has come to be used pejoratively, with strong connotations of criminality and disregard for other people's property and has thus become highly stigmatized, which is why many people prefer to avoid it.

It needs to be remembered, though, that Roma is a generic term and includes diverse groups, each of which has its own traditions, languages and lifestyles (Sarafian *et al.*, 2024).

The related term of 'Traveller' (note the capital T to denote that it is being used in a specialist sense, rather than generically to anyone who travels) also encompasses various groups, including Irish and Scottish Travellers known for their nomadic lifestyles (hence the term 'Traveller'). While 'Traveller' broadly signifies those who are part of a nomadic tradition, not all people who identify as Roma are Travellers and not all Travellers identify as Roma. So, while the two terms overlap to a certain extent, we should be careful not to make the mistake of regarding them as synonymous.

We need to remember that these terms are not merely labels or reference points; they are also a key part of the basis for the constant and enduring challenges of marginalization; health, education and employment inequalities; social exclusion; and suspicion, mistrust and hostility (Khanna, 2024).

The stigma attached to such groups contributes to significant levels of discrimination and thus oppression. For example, children from these communities can be seen to lose out in terms of educational achievement (Marcus, 2019). Irish Travellers are recognized as one of the most oppressed ethnic groups in Ireland and the effects of discrimination are to be found in such social indicators as health, education and socioeconomic status compared to the general population (McGinnity *et al.*, 2021).

Social exclusion and associated disadvantages faced by young people are known to lead to risky and socially problematic behaviours, such as substance abuse. The Roma and Traveller communities are no exception to this. Poor literacy levels and a lack of access to education about drugs and related services can be seen to compound the problem and increase the risks involved (Hout and Connor, 2008). Part of the problem is the relative invisibility of Romani and Traveller peoples in education curricula or other resources geared towards combating stereotypes and discriminatory assumptions (Cavaliero, 2020).

In terms of PCS analysis, prejudicial views towards Romani and Traveller people at the personal level are rife. This reflects the stigma and stereotypes that feature strongly in cultural representations of such people as potentially dangerous 'outsiders'. In turn, such narratives feed into and are fed by structural factors, such as the challenges on the part of the powers that be involved in controlling and taxing largely mobile communities. Unless and until, positive steps are taken to educate the general public about Romani and Traveller people as part of a commitment to equality, diversity and inclusion, they will remain marginalized and thereby face discrimination in myriad ways.

Eastern Europeans

The inclusion in the European Union (EU) in 2004 of people from Eastern European countries in the days when the United Kingdom was a member state in the EU was not welcomed by certain sectors of the British public. One of the privileges of EU membership is the right to live and work in any of the member states without the need for a visa (known as 'freedom of movement'). A large number of people from Poland and other Eastern European countries came to the UK, an influx that triggered racist reactions across wide sectors of the population.

What was not taken into account by those who held such racist views was that the immigrants were filling labour shortages and paying taxes to help fund the UK Government. They were not, as some claimed, a drain on the economy but, of course, misinformation is a common feature of racist thinking.

TIP! Be very careful about how you interpret information in the media about any group of immigrants. Discriminatory assumptions are very common, sometimes openly prejudicial, sometimes much more subtle.

Racist sentiments were broadly in evidence in the build up and aftermath of the referendum which led to the UK leaving the European Union (commonly known as Brexit).

Research undertaken by Tereshchenko *et al.* (2019) highlights how Eastern European settlers experience what they termed 'marginal whiteness' due to being perceived as outsiders. This illustrates a key message of this chapter, namely that racism is not simply a matter of white or black skin. The racism involved can be understood as, in part, cultural racism, but with the added dimension of linguistic differences forming a basis of discrimination for some people.

Lulle *et al.* (2017) noted the emotional repercussions of the Brexit referendum on Eastern European migrants. The divide between British citizens and incomers increased feelings of being unwelcome (see the discussion of 'othering' in Chapter 9). Xenophobia is the term used to refer to hostility towards people perceived as 'foreigners', and this has clearly been in evidence towards Eastern European migrants. For example, Rzepnikowska (2018) found an increase in racism and xenophobia towards Polish migrants following the Brexit vote. Shared European citizenship and identity seemed to count for little to very many people.

There is also evidence to suggest that Eastern Europeans additionally face discrimination in the labour market, often being seen as expendable and as suitable only for low-paid, unstable jobs (Kotýnková, 2020). This can create a problematic feedback loop, in the sense that their employment status feeds the stereotype that they are second-class citizens and the stereotype then acts as a barrier to better-paid higher-status employment. They are largely 'locked in' to low-status employment.

Although predominantly white, their ethnic status has become racialized, thereby leaving them open to racism. There is research that shows that they are also at an increased risk of mental health problems due to the discrimination they encounter, combined with poor access to supportive services (Madden *et al.*, 2017; Phung *et al.*, 2020).

This type of racism tends to receive far less attention than what is traditionally thought of as racism. We need to be careful, therefore, in our professional and management practices to ensure that we are not missing instances of racism and are therefore leaving ourselves less well equipped to be engaging appropriately in anti-racism.

Internal colonialism

We discussed earlier the significance of colonialism and its role in slavery. The British Empire, along with other colonial powers such as Portugal and the Netherlands, played a major part in conquering other nations, exploiting their natural resources and, worst of all, condemning millions of people to a life of unpaid servitude a long way from their families, their communities and their cultures. Enslavement was an overt act of brutal and heartless mistreatment of fellow human beings. The story of this shameful chapter of British history is well known (Williams, 2022), although perhaps not as well known as it should be.

However, there is another dimension of colonialism that has received far less attention and that is what is known as 'internal colonialism'. This refers to how Welsh people were historically subjugated, their language and culture vilified and subject to determined and sustained efforts towards their eradication. For example, in the 19th century, children were punished for speaking Welsh

(Griffiths, 2021) as part of official efforts to make English the sole language to be used in Wales – language, of course, being a symbol of power and dominance.

Griffiths (2021) comments on an 1848 report on the state of religious education in Wales in which there is ample evidence of poverty that could explain the poor quality of learning. However, the report concluded that: 'the problem inherent in the country's education system was not poverty, or low standards, or a lack of teacher training, but the Welsh language' (p. 14). There is a direct parallel here with the imperialist control mechanism of establishing control in part by replacing local languages with the language of the conqueror. The tendency to treat the Welsh language as a problem rather than an asset is now far less in evidence, although it has not disappeared altogether. The resilience of Welsh language and culture has proven strong enough to withstand the colonial onslaught.

The basic idea of internal colonialism stems from the work of Antonio Gramsci (1998), the sociologist and political thinker renowned for introducing the idea of 'hegemony' – control not through force, but through ideology, the suppression of local languages being part of this. Hechter (1999) applied the idea to the 'Celtic fringe' – that is, the Celtic nations around the British Isles that have historically been marginalized by the advances of Anglo-Saxon peoples. The legacy of this is still to be found in modern policy characterized by cultural dominance and economic deprivation (Ferretti, 2017). For example, the HS2 project to improve high-speed rail links between the south and north of England brings no benefit to Wales, but Welsh funds are still being used to finance it, while the Welsh railway system leaves much to be desired.

As a personal example of colonialist thinking towards Wales, I was once at a high-powered meeting in London when, during a coffee break, an employee of the organization concerned said to me: 'I've been impressed with you. I wasn't expecting someone from Wales to be so intelligent and articulate'. He seemed to be totally oblivious to the implications of his comment (until I pointed them out to him). Sadly, this is not an isolated incident. This assumption of inferiority is not limited to Wales, as it applies across the Celtic fringe. I have heard, for example, numerous references to Scotland and Ireland as 'backwaters'.

Hechter drew on the concept of core-periphery within a nation. He argued that processes parallel with the colonialism associated with the rise of the British Empire can also be seen to operate *within* a country. In Britain, the core would be England, especially London and the southeast where most of the wealth is to be found, and the periphery would be those areas dominated and exploited by the power centre at the core: notably Wales, Scotland and Northern Ireland (the Republic of Ireland having at one time already become a colony of Great Britain before achieving independence).

The consequences of this core-periphery power dynamic include economic exploitation and uneven development (hence the concept of 'levelling up' embraced at one time by the then Conservative government – in principle if not in practice – as a process of fairer redistribution of resources and opportunities). Hechter argued that the British state's economic policies and associated investment activities favoured the core, thereby discriminating against the periphery at a structural level (supported by the stereotypes at a cultural level of London and the southeast as 'vibrant' and other parts of the UK as weak and backward – consider how the term 'provincial' is, at root, purely a descriptive term but is often used pejoratively to mean unsophisticated and underdeveloped).

Similar examples of Hechter's model can be found beyond the UK – for example, Spain (Catalonia and the Basque Country), Canada (Québec) and elsewhere. Although the relationship between the UK and the Republic of Ireland cannot be regarded as *internal* colonialism, as they are two separate countries, prior to the establishment of Ireland as a republic in 1949, the same issues applied. Indeed, the history of the impetus for Irish independence can be seen as in large part a rejection of internal colonialism. Campaigns for Scottish and Welsh independence can also be understood to have similar roots – a desire to move away from a core-periphery model where the power is largely to be found in the core, leaving the periphery disadvantaged and even stigmatized.

The concept of cultural hegemony, as articulated by Antonio Gramsci, offers a valuable framework for understanding how dominant English narratives have consistently functioned to subordinate Welsh and Scottish national identities (Ferretti, 2017). This dynamic is exemplified in the concept of 'anglocentrism' which refers to the tendency to interpret the world, including its history, culture and language, primarily from an English perspective – often assuming that perspective to be central, superior or universally applicable. Such a lens frequently frames global or British events through an English viewpoint, thereby reinforcing a conception of British history as essentially English history. This framing serves to diminish the visibility and significance of Welsh and Scottish contributions and experiences. For example, there have been television programmes about *British* history which only mention Scotland in relation to England and have little or nothing to say about Wales.

In the cultural sphere, Welsh and Scottish identities have often been subjected to stereotyping or trivialization within British media representations. English cultural norms are routinely presented as the default or standard across the UK, overshadowing distinctively Welsh, Scottish and Northern Irish traditions, literature and religious practices. Similarly, Celtic fringe contributions to fields such as science, politics and the arts are frequently underrepresented or subsumed into a broader 'British' identity that implicitly privileges Englishness. As such, anglocentrism has played a substantial role in the marginalization of Wales, Scotland and Northern Ireland within the political, cultural, and historical narratives of the UK.

What we are seeing, then, is the legacy of colonialism within the specific context of *internal* colonialism. The historic picture has created complex multi-dimensional power dynamics that are distinctive in some ways, but which follow general patterns in others (dominance-subordination relations, ideology serving the powerful, systemic discrimination being presented as isolated instances of personal prejudice and so on).

Irish people

The term 'Ireland' is a contested one. The Island of Ireland is a geographical term, but when we consider Ireland from a sociopolitical perspective, the position becomes more complex. This is because, at one time Ireland became a colony of Great Britain, creating the extended nation of the United Kingdom of Great Britain and Ireland. Following many years of political rebellion, most of Ireland separated from Britain to become an independent country. However, the six counties to the North East of Ireland were not included and continued to be part of the UK (now renamed as the United Kingdom of Great Britain and Northern Ireland).

Discrimination against Irish people in the UK has deep historical roots and continues to influence the lived experiences of many individuals today. For professionals working in the human services and managers across all sectors, an understanding of this history – and its ongoing effects – is essential for promoting equality, diversity and inclusion and culturally sensitive practice.

The historical division between Northern Ireland and the Republic of Ireland was fundamentally shaped by identity. The Republic is a predominantly Catholic country, while the six counties that remained part of the UK were historically Protestant (albeit to a lesser degree, given recent demographics). The tensions created by this division played a key role in fuelling the conflict known as the 'Troubles', which will be explored further in Chapter 8. These religious and political dynamics continue to influence the social positioning of Irish people, families and communities in the UK.

For present purposes, I am using the term Irish as an inclusive term to refer to people from both the Republic and from Northern Ireland. This approach recognizes that both groups have experienced discrimination and that shared aspects of identity, history and experience are relevant to inclusive and respectful professional practice.

Irish migration to Britain during the 19th century must be understood in the context of colonial narratives that positioned Irish people as an inferior race. These damaging perceptions have not disappeared entirely. Corbally (2009a, 2009b) notes that such attitudes persist today, often manifesting through the continued circulation of anti-Irish jokes based on harmful stereotypes of low intelligence. While presented as humour ('taking the Mick'), these portrayals carry the potential to reinforce stigma, undermine self-worth and shape internalized perceptions of cultural inferiority. For practitioners and managers, it is important to recognize how everyday language and humour can contribute to a wider pattern of discrimination, albeit often unintentionally.

Reflective moment

How would you feel if the ethnic or linguistic group you are part of were the constant butt of unkind humour? What effects might it have on you?

Research supports the view that Irish people in the UK have been and continue to be subject to discrimination. For example, McGinnity and Lunn (2011) highlight how favouritism and unconscious bias often result in the exclusion of Irish individuals, along with other minority ethnic groups, from fair treatment. These biases are deeply rooted in colonial histories but now often operate in subtle and systemic ways – through assumptions, institutional practices and the absence of recognition in equality and diversity frameworks.

The Great Famine (1845–1852) was a significant turning point, leading to the emigration of more than a million Irish people to Britain. At that time, the widespread failure of the potato crop left large sections of the population facing starvation. Irish migrants arriving in Britain encountered severe hostility, substandard housing, poorly paid work, and open prejudice. Explicit discrimination was commonplace – signs such as "No Irish, No Blacks, No Dogs" were a feature of public establishments and lodging houses well into the 20th century (Hickman and Walter, 1997).

Over time, Irish people in Britain came to be associated with negative stereotypes – being portrayed as heavy drinkers, violent and lacking intelligence. These representations were reinforced through the media and other cultural channels. As Garner (2007) argues, this constitutes a form of *cultural racism* in which Irish people – despite being racially categorized as white – were subjected to exclusion and discrimination. Importantly, anti-Irish racism has often been treated as less serious or less harmful than other forms of racism, an attitude that still lingers in some professional and organizational cultures.

Although explicit hostility has declined in recent decades, discrimination against Irish people has not been fully eradicated. Research by Hickman *et al.* (2005) found that people of Irish heritage in Britain continue to be marginalized and are frequently left out of equality, diversity and inclusion policies. A lack of inclusion in ethnic monitoring systems contributes to the invisibility of this group in service planning, resource allocation and equality initiatives.

Older Irish people are particularly vulnerable, with studies showing that they experience disproportionately high levels of poverty and ill-health compared to the wider population (Tilki *et al.*, 2009). For both managers and practitioners, this highlights the importance of recognizing the significance of cultural background, migration history and patterns of discrimination when assessing need and designing services.

'Oriental' peoples

Racism towards East and Southeast Asian (ESEA) communities is one such area. Often overlooked in mainstream diversity agendas, this form of racism has deep historical roots and continues to shape experiences of marginalization and exclusion in contemporary society.

The marginalization of ESEA communities is rooted in the historical processes of colonialism we have already mentioned, as well as what is known as orientalist thinking (that is, thinking that is based on distorted stereotypical understandings of the peoples of the East). The term 'oriental' is now largely considered outdated and inappropriate. It originated within western imperial discourses that characterized Asian societies as mysterious, exotic and inferior (Said, 1978). These ideas were used to justify political domination and economic exploitation.

British colonial interventions in Asia, particularly through events such as the Opium Wars and trade with China, reinforced racialized representations of Asian peoples as servile, dangerous and thus alien (Yeh, 2014). Such portrayals were disseminated through literature, the media and public discourse, leaving a distorted and discriminatory legacy on British perceptions of ESEA individuals to this day.

Contemporary racism towards ESEA communities can be seen as another form of cultural racism, where people are presented as fundamentally different based on perceived cultural characteristics.

One example of this is the 'model minority' stereotype, with ESEA people perceived as industrious, compliant and academically successful (Chou and Feagin, 2015). While this may initially appear to be a positive characterization, closer consideration reveals it to have harmful consequences. It can obscure the diversity of experience within ESEA communities by 'homogenizing' the different subgroups, conceal socioeconomic inequalities and lay the foundations for disregarding claims of racism.

In addition, negative stereotypes also persist, including the depiction of ESEA men as passive or emasculated and ESEA women as exoticized and hypersexualized. Such objectifications reduce individuals to racialized stereotypes and thereby contribute to their social exclusion (Ng *et al.*, 2021).

The COVID-19 pandemic marked a significant escalation in anti-Asian racism, not only in the UK but also globally. The association of the virus with China led to a surge in racialized abuse against people perceived to be Chinese or of broader East and Southeast Asian heritage. Public Health England (2020) reported a notable increase in hate crimes against these communities during the early stages of the pandemic.

Politicized language such as the 'Chinese virus' and 'Kung Flu' oversimplified a complex situation and contributed to Asian communities being stigmatized, invoking longstanding ideas of disease and foreignness (Cheng and Agyepong, 2021). Advocacy organizations, such as End the Virus of Racism (2021), have highlighted instances of verbal harassment, physical assault and social exclusion. Victims often reported a lack of support and a lack of recognition within broader anti-racist campaigns and discourses (Khan, 2022).

These developments highlight the need to be alert to emerging manifestations of racism, particularly when they are triggered by global events and amplified through the media and political rhetoric.

A key feature of anti-ESEA racism is its relative invisibility within institutional frameworks. Despite evidence of discrimination, ESEA people are frequently underrepresented in discussions of race and inequality. In many organizations, diversity monitoring does not distinguish between different Asian communities, thereby obscuring the specific experiences of ESEA groups and making it difficult to develop targeted interventions.

A genuine commitment to anti-racism requires us to address racism in all its forms. With regard to ESEA communities, this means a historically informed and culturally sensitive approach that is consistent with intersectionality. It also means ensuring that:

- Cultural competency training addresses the histories, identities and experiences of ESEA people. This includes understanding the legacy of orientalism and the persistence of stereotypes.
- Monitoring and reporting systems distinguish between different Asian subgroups to ensure that disparities affecting ESEA communities are made visible and can be addressed effectively.
- Clear mechanisms for reporting and responding to racist incidents are in place in all relevant settings. These protocols should acknowledge the specific dynamics of anti-ESEA racism.
- ESEA people are meaningfully included in decision-making processes, diversity working groups and consultation exercises to ensure that their experiences inform policy and practice.
- Critically reflective practice is used to challenge stereotypes and discriminatory assumptions about ESEA people. This includes recognizing the diversity and complexity within ESEA communities.

Racism towards East and Southeast Asian communities remains an under-recognized but significant form of discrimination in the UK. Rooted in colonial history and perpetuated through cultural stereotypes, it manifests today in both overt hostility and institutional exclusion. Recognizing and addressing this form of racism is therefore essential.

Indigenous peoples

As we noted earlier, a genuine commitment to anti-racism involves a sustained and critical engagement with the histories, cultures, and present-day realities of those peoples subject to racism. This applies too to indigenous peoples, by which I mean Native American communities, Canadian First Nations, Australian Aborigines and Torres Strait Islanders, Māori, Inuit and so on.

For centuries, colonial systems and racist ideologies have systematically marginalized, dispossessed and inflicted profound harm upon indigenous communities. We need to recognize the entrenched structures that sustain this form of racism and the cultural stereotypes and discriminatory assumptions that both reflect and reinforce those structures.

While acknowledging the uniqueness and distinctive circumstances – past and present – of each group, we can identify overarching principles for respectful, culturally competent and effective anti-racist practice.

Once again, we are faced with the consequences of colonialism and empire building. And once again those consequences include social, economic and health inequalities experienced by minority groups, in this case indigenous peoples. Colonization, as a global phenomenon, entailed the forceful appropriation of ancestral lands, the suppression once again of local languages and cultural practices, the forced removal of children from their families, and the imposition of foreign legal and political systems (Alfred and Corntassel, 2005; Moreton-Robinson, 2015; Truth and Reconciliation Commission of Canada, 2015). These processes were legitimized and sustained by racist ideologies that presented indigenous peoples as inferior and their ways of life as impediments to what was seen as progress.

The legacy of these historical travesties continues to be apparent to the present day. The following examples highlight the destructiveness of colonialism for indigenous peoples.

Dispossession of land

The loss of traditional territories has disrupted cultural practices, diminished economic self-sufficiency and weakened spiritual connections to the land (a very important consideration to many indigenous peoples). In North America, the acquisition of land by European settlers steadily forced the indigenous peoples into smaller enclaves and eventually into designated reservations. The result of this process of marginalization was a significant transfer of natural resources from the original residents to the incomers. Witgen (2022) uses the telling phrase of 'the political economy of plunder' to refer to this situation.

Cox (2022) makes a similar point in stating that:

> Before the arrival of the White explorers, treasure seekers, and traders, the Americas had many thriving cultures many of whom had learned to live peacefully with one another. … Seeing themselves as 'discovering' the Americas as well as bringing a far superior culture and way of life upon those living in the Americas. They also believed that the resources they found in the Americas were there for the taking, … Little regard was given to the damage that their acts of greed were doing to those already living in the Americas.
>
> (p. 71)

Despite these ravages, Treuer (2019) is keen to emphasize, today's Native Americans remain proud of their culture and heritage and show great resilience in the face of considerable sociopolitical challenges.

In Australia, a parallel process occurred. The continent was deemed to be 'terra nullius' – that is, no one's land, showing complete disregard for the rights or wellbeing of the Aboriginal residents. Lindquist (2007) outlines the ideology underpinning this form of land seizure:

> Empty land. Uninhabited land. Land that will soon be uninhabited because it is populated by inferior races, condemned by the laws of nature to die out. Land where the original inhabitants are, or can be soon rendered, so few in number as to be negligible.

> (p. 4)

This contempt towards fellow human beings was historically a characteristic feature of colonialism and remains a common element of racist thinking.

Cultural genocide

The adoption of assimilationist policies – such as the setting up of residential schools in Canada and the United States and the forced removal of the 'Stolen Generations' in Australia – resulted in profound and extensive damage in relation to:

■ *Indigenous languages* Griffiths (2021, p. 4) describes the English language as 'one of a handful of super tongues, which bulldoze others in their path'. Colonialism placed pressure on a wide range of languages, with some facing extinction as a result of the dominance of English. Similar processes occurred as a result of Spanish, Portuguese, French and Dutch as colonial languages. As we noted earlier, language is a key dimension of identity, and so the loss of a language is not simply a technical matter of adopting a different language – there are significant challenges in terms of personal and cultural identity.

■ *Kinship systems* European patterns of family relationships are not universal. However, as with language usage, imperialist pressures brought about changes in family structures and systems, with a shift of focus from broader, community-based patterns of kinship to a greater role for the nuclear family, with a potential loss of community resources and support.

■ *Cultural transmission* The survival of cultures depends on the successful transmission from one generation to the next of values and beliefs at an abstract level and rituals and ceremonies at a more directly practical level. The influence of dominant colonial cultures can interfere with such mechanisms of transmission and also create intergenerational conflicts as each new generation moves further away from the old traditions that have defined their culture (and thus in part their identity) and more towards the 'modern' folkways associated with the colonial powers.

■ *Socioeconomic inequality* Indigenous communities frequently experience disproportionately high levels of poverty, unemployment, substandard housing and reduced access to education and healthcare. These can be seen as the consequences of structural factors that privilege the rights and needs of the powerful majority at the expense of the indigenous minority.

■ *Health inequalities* Colonialism has contributed to significantly poorer health outcomes for indigenous peoples, including higher rates of chronic illness, mental health problems and substance misuse. These can be seen to be, in large part, the consequences of socioeconomic inequality and the associated social problems. A further knock-on effect is a decrease in lifespan (Thompson *et al.*, 2012).

■ *Over-representation in the criminal justice system* The combination of the detrimental effects of the inequalities indigenous people face and institutionalized racism in policing and legal institutions has led to the disproportionate surveillance, criminalization and imprisonment of indigenous people (Thurber *et al.*, 2021). Links between inequality and social problems, including crime, are well documented (Thompson, 2017a). The promotion of social justice therefore has an important part to play in reducing crime and tackling other social problems.

The 'Stolen Generations' refers to the policy enacted in Australia between approximately 1910 and 1970 which involved placing lighterskinned aboriginal children with white families in a misguided (and profoundly racist) effort to 'breed out' the blackness as far as possible. The residential schools served a similar purpose, clearly based on a white supremacist ideology geared towards eradicating aboriginal cultures and replacing them with the dominant ideology of the power elite.

By considering each of these issues overall, we can identify three important themes:

■ These elements interact and influence each other, often compounding the detrimental effects (another example of intersectionality). They are part of a broader picture of inequality, discrimination and oppression.

■ Underpinning this picture is a complex set of power dynamics. Colonialism is, of course, based on the exercise of power in subduing other nations and cultures in order to benefit from their resources as part of the process of empire building. While this is clearly significant historically, we should not lose sight of the fact that the impact of colonialism is still to be felt to this day in a number of ways (Sanghera, 2021).

■ Alienation, the sense of not belonging, not being valued or welcome can be linked with each of the issues raised here. Alienation has a two-way relationship with power. It arises from the misuse or abuse of power that creates a sense of powerlessness and that powerlessness is a significant source of alienation.

Once again, we find ourselves in complex territory that highlights that an understanding of racism based simply on personal prejudice is far from adequate for making sense of what is happening and thus for planning how best to respond to the challenges involved.

At the heart of anti-racist practice with indigenous peoples is the need to recognize and respect their inherent sovereignty and their right to self-determination. These rights are enshrined in international law, most notably in the *United Nations Declaration on the Rights of Indigenous Peoples* (UNDRIP, 2007), which articulates the right of indigenous peoples to freely determine their political status and to pursue their own economic, social and cultural development. This is, in a very real sense, a counterbalance to colonialism, an affirmation of the rights of such minority groups to go beyond the restrictions originally imposed by colonial settlement and the relations of dominance it established.

Developing an effective anti-racist approach requires us to critically examine the ways in which organizations perpetuate racism against indigenous peoples through institutionalized practices, assumptions and language use. This includes:

- *Tackling bias*: In PCS analysis terms, indigenous peoples are subject to a number of inaccurate and harmful stereotypes at the C level of culture. These are deeply ingrained through longstanding media representations that do not do justice to the people concerned. There is therefore much to be gained from critically examining such biases and taking the necessary steps to eradicate them.
- *Challenging deficit-based thinking*: The problems highlighted above can be attributed in large part to wider sociopolitical factors, but they are often presented ideologically as character flaws in the individuals or communities concerned. Such inaccurate assumptions then form the basis of discriminatory attitudes. Consequently, it is important not only to avoid such deficit-based thinking, but also to challenge it whenever we can.
- *Promoting change*: This involves not only how we speak and behave, but also how we can play a part, individually and collectively in influencing policy and strategy development, press for appropriate education and training, and so on. This can involve working with like-minded people, both within and outside indigenous communities and supporting initiatives arising from indigenous communities.

This is by no means an exhaustive list, but it should be enough to form a basis for addressing racism against indigenous peoples in whatever form it may take.

The caste system

The caste system, as used in the Indian subcontinent and Indian communities across the world, is an ancient system of social stratification. It basically amounts to dividing people into a hierarchy of prestige and status. It ranges from the Brahmins (the priest and scholar class) at the peak to the Dalits (formerly referred to as 'Untouchables') at the bottom. In between are Kshatriyas (warriors), Vaishyas (merchants) and Shudras (labourers).

It is similar in some ways to a class system, but is much more rigid, in the sense that, while there is some degree of social mobility in class terms, caste is much more fixed. It is, in effect, a racialized hierarchy, in the sense that it assigns people to a status according to perceived difference (based on heredity), rather than according to merit, achievement or contribution.

It is traditionally associated with Hinduism but has some degree of influence over major religious communities in South Asia, including Muslims, Sikhs, Christians and Buddhists.

The caste system affects access to resources, educational opportunities, occupations, education and even where people can live. Although India formally abolished 'untouchability' under Article 17 of the Indian Constitution and introduced affirmative action policies in 1950, caste-based discrimination persists in both overt and subtle forms.

As we have noted, understandings of racism are not simply about skin colour or other biological factors; it encompasses socially constructed categories that organize people hierarchically based on perceived differences (Fredrickson, 2015). Caste, like race, operates as a closed system of ascribed status. In PCS terms, it can be seen to operate at a structural level to produce significant levels of inequality and disadvantage; at a cultural level, negative stereotypes bring stigma which, in turn, can give rise to alienation with consequent impacts on self-esteem and self-respect and thus a higher risk of depression or other mental health problems

In 2001, at the United Nations World Conference Against Racism in Durban, caste-based discrimination was officially recognized as analogous to racial discrimination. Scholars such as Ambedkar (2014) and Yengde (2018) have argued that caste oppression mirrors the patterns of anti-Black racism and settler colonialism, including dehumanization, segregation, and violence.

Caste-based discrimination is not confined to South Asia. Migrant communities in the UK, the United States, Canada, and other regions have carried caste identities and prejudices with them. A report by Zwick-Maitreyi *et al* (2018) found that 67% of Dalit respondents in the United States faced caste-based workplace discrimination, and 25% reported physical assault because of their caste.

> **TIP!** Beware of making the mistake of assuming that caste-related issues apply only in India. They can potentially be found in communities with Indian heritage in various parts of the world.

In the UK, the issue of caste discrimination has gained legal and political attention. The Employment Appeals Tribunal in *Tirkey v. Chandok* (2014) recognized caste discrimination as a form of racial discrimination under the Equality Act 2010, even in the absence of explicit caste provisions in the law. Although the UK government declined to make caste a specific protected characteristic, the ruling set an important precedent.

Returning to the important concept of intersectionality, we should be careful to note that caste does not operate in isolation; it intersects with gender and class in ways that compound marginalization. For example, Dalit women in particular are subjected to multiple layers of discrimination – patriarchal, caste related and economic. They are more likely to face sexual violence, exclusion from education, and hazardous or exploitative labour conditions (Sabharwal and Sonalkar, 2015).

This intersectionality is crucial for human services professionals to understand. A Dalit woman working in a cleaning job, for example, may face discrimination not only as a low-income worker but also due to ingrained cultural beliefs about purity, pollution and hierarchy. Addressing such forms of injustice requires an integrated approach that considers the cumulative effects of multiple identities.

In addition, the caste system continues to shape access to education, employment and social capital. Despite affirmative action policies (referred to as 'reservations' in India), Dalits and other marginalized caste groups are often underrepresented in higher education and professional sectors. They face bullying in schools, microaggressions in the workplace and barriers to promotion and leadership roles (Thorat and Newman, 2010).

For international students and professionals from South Asian backgrounds, caste identities can affect interpersonal relationships, mentorship opportunities and a sense of institutional belonging. As a result, discrimination may remain hidden or unspoken, yet still profoundly shape outcomes.

Caste-based discrimination is maintained not only through sociopolitical structures, but also through cultural norms, institutional practices, language use and everyday behaviour. Marriage practices remain strongly caste bound, with families prioritizing 'caste purity' in arranged marriages. Surnames often indicate caste, leading to stereotyping or exclusion. Ritual pollution beliefs persist in rural and urban settings, affecting where people can live, eat and worship.

Media representations also contribute to caste-based discrimination by erasing Dalit voices or reinforcing stereotypes. Positive depictions of Dalit lives are rare, while narratives reflecting the interests of the dominant groups are normalized. This absence of representation further contributes to the invisibility and marginalization of caste-oppressed communities.

Professionals working in social care, education, health, housing and justice sectors as well as managers in all settings need to develop awareness of caste as a form of racism. This includes:

- *Cultural competence*: Training relating to the caste system and its contemporary impact can help practitioners and managers understand the nuances of social hierarchy in South Asian contexts. Caste awareness should be integrated into diversity and inclusion training.
- *Anti-discrimination policies*: Organizations should adopt explicit anti-caste discrimination policies, especially in contexts with significant South Asian

representation. Recruitment, disciplinary processes and service delivery protocols should be reviewed for caste bias.

■ *Safeguarding and whistleblowing*: Individuals experiencing caste-based bullying or exclusion should have access to safe reporting mechanisms. This is particularly important in educational institutions and workplaces.

■ *Advocacy and representation*: Increasing the representation of caste-oppressed individuals in leadership roles is key to addressing systemic inequities. Encouraging dialogue and storytelling from these communities can also help challenge stigma.

■ *Community engagement*: Service providers working with South Asian communities must engage with diverse caste groups, including grassroots Dalit-led organizations, to ensure inclusive programming and consultation.

The caste system constitutes a deeply racialized structure of inequality that continues to shape lives in India and globally. Its intersection with race, class and gender exacerbates its impact, leading to widespread human rights violations and social exclusion. Recognizing caste discrimination as a form of racism is a necessary step for human services professionals and managers who are committed to social justice and dignity in their work. Addressing caste-related discrimination requires both structural reform and cultural change – within institutions, communities and individual practice.

Finally, in terms of caste, Wilkerson (2020) offers a thought-provoking discussion in which she describes three historic incidences of caste: not only India, as we have discussed, but also Nazi Germany in which Jewish people were treated as a form of subhuman caste and contemporary America where caste largely takes the form of race, upheld by a discourse of white supremacy. Caste can therefore be understood to be a concept that can be applied more broadly than is commonly the case, rooted as it is in a sense of human hierarchy that has no natural or biological basis in reality.

Colourism

Colourism, a term introduced by author and activist Alice Walker (1982), refers to a form of discrimination in which individuals are treated differently based on the relative lightness or darkness of their skin tone. Distinct from racism, colourism operates both within and between racial and ethnic groups, privileging lighter skin tones and reinforcing social hierarchies rooted in colonialism, patriarchy, and classism.

It is important to understand the implications of colourism in order to address its impact within organizational practices and service delivery. The issue of colourism applies not only to India itself, but also to Indian communities to be found in many other countries across the world.

Colourism in the Indian subcontinent is deeply embedded in historical structures. While caste hierarchies and regional diversity pre-date colonial rule,

British colonialism intensified associations between whiteness and social superiority. British governance strategies and cultural hegemony embedded the notion that lighter skin was synonymous with modernity, civility and intelligence (Parameswaran and Cardoza, 2009). These values were internalized through educational systems, employment practices and media depictions that persist to this day in both subtle and overt forms.

Pre-colonial beliefs also contributed to the problem. In several Asian societies, fair skin was historically associated with wealth and status, since those who did not perform outdoor labour retained lighter complexions. However, colonial and capitalist systems amplified these class distinctions and translated them into racialized hierarchies.

Comparable patterns are found in other parts of the world. In the United States, slavery and segregation created internalized colour hierarchies among African Americans (Hunter, 2007). Similarly, in Latin America, colonial caste systems institutionalized a preference for lighter skin, while in East Asian societies skin lightness has long symbolized beauty and refinement, though often within a class framework. Interestingly, when I was in India, I noticed that glamorous women featured heavily in advertising and each and every one of them had much lighter skin than the majority of Indian people. Lighter skin shades were clearly valorized.

In modern India, colourism manifests across multiple domains, including the media, advertising, employment, and the institution of marriage. The skin-lightening industry, worth billions of rupees, thrives on perpetuating the belief that fair skin enhances attractiveness, success and confidence. Brands such as Fair & Lovely (now Glow & Lovely) have historically disseminated narratives equating dark skin with failure and fair skin with transformation and achievement (Mishra, 2015).

Similarly, marriage continues to be a significant site of colour-based discrimination. Matrimonial advertisements routinely express preferences for 'fair' brides or grooms, underscoring how skin tone remains a determinant of perceived desirability. In film and television, lighter-skinned actors are overrepresented in lead roles, while darker-skinned individuals are often cast in roles that reinforce stereotypes.

As we might expect, colourism intersects with other forms of social inequality, including gender, caste and class. Women face disproportionate pressure to conform to fairness ideals due to their social value being closely tied to physical appearance and suitability for marriage (Glenn, 2008). This can lead to psychological consequences such as low self-esteem, internalized shame, alienation and even the use of harmful skin-lightening products.

Although skin tone does not correlate directly with caste, the legacy of caste-based occupational segregation – particularly in rural and labour-intensive contexts – has led to persistent associations between darker skin and lower status. Dalit and Adivasi individuals, in particular, often experience compounded discrimination based on caste and skin tone (Thorat and Newman, 2010).

Colourism is a global phenomenon. In African-American communities in the United States, studies have shown that lighter-skinned individuals often experience advantages in education, employment and the criminal justice system (Monk, 2014). Similarly, in many Latin American countries, political and economic power remains concentrated among lighter-skinned populations. In addition, Apartheid era South Africa had three legal categories of people: white, coloured and black, with 'coloured' people being intermediate between white and black in terms of rights and status.

In East Asia, including China, Japan and South Korea, pale skin is historically associated with femininity, purity and social prestige. Although often rooted in class, these biases have been commercialized in the global beauty industry, with widespread use of skin-lightening products and strong social stigma attached to tanned or darker skin (Li *et al*., 2008).

The media play a critical role in perpetuating colourist ideologies. Films, advertisements and digital content often promote narrow standards of beauty that equate light skin with desirability and success. These portrayals not only reflect societal attitudes but also reinforce them by normalizing exclusionary practices and marginalizing darker-skinned individuals (Hunter, 2005).

Globalization has extended the reach of Eurocentric beauty standards, while also facilitating the export of colourist messaging from dominant markets. Nevertheless, social media platforms have emerged as spaces for counter-narratives, enabling grassroots campaigns that challenge colourism and promote inclusive representations of beauty and success.

Resistance to colourism is gaining momentum across many societies. In India, the 'Dark Is Beautiful' campaign, initiated by the NGO Women of Worth, challenges fairness-based beauty ideals and advocates for self-acceptance and media accountability. The rebranding of Fair & Lovely following public criticism, although contested, reflects increased corporate awareness of these issues (Naidoo, 2020).

Globally, the resurgence of the Black Lives Matter movement has reignited conversations about internalized racism, including the significance of skin tone hierarchies. Activists, artists and educators continue to play a key role in dismantling colourism through education, cultural production and policy advocacy.

From a professional practice point of view, it is important to be able to recognize and challenge colourism whenever it is encountered. This involves a number of steps, such as:

- *Awareness and self-reflection* Practitioners must critically examine their own attitudes and biases towards skin tone and understand how these may affect decision making.
- *Equitable service delivery* Professionals should ensure that policies and practices do not reinforce colourist assumptions, particularly in areas such as recruitment, health care, education and marketing.

- *Representation and inclusion* Institutions must actively work to represent individuals of diverse skin tones in leadership, promotional materials and organizational narratives.
- *Support and advocacy* Providing psychological support to those affected by colourism – especially young people – is essential. This includes promoting self-acceptance and challenging negative stereotypes in therapeutic, educational and community settings.
- *Policy reform* Managers and professionals should advocate for anti-discrimination policies that explicitly address colourism, including anti-bias training, inclusive hiring and the monitoring of workplace culture.

Colourism is a deeply embedded form of social discrimination that privileges lighter skin and marginalizes darker-skinned individuals. Rooted in historical structures of caste, colonialism and patriarchy, it continues to affect access to resources, opportunities and self-worth. For professionals in human services and managers in any setting, recognizing and addressing colourism is a critical step towards fostering equitable, inclusive and socially just environments. This requires not only individual reflection and professional development, but also organizational commitment to representation, policy change and cultural transformation.

Key point

Once again, we find skin colour, which has no intrinsic value, being constructed as socially significant, with detrimental consequences for minority groups and some degree of benefit and privilege for the majority.

Rural people

The English word 'peasant' derives from the French 'paysan', which simply refers to a country dweller. The fact that it has developed pejorative connotations illustrates that people from rural communities are yet another group prone to being stereotyped and discriminated against on the grounds of socially constructed differences.

The idea that city dwellers tend to be seen as modern, sophisticated and forward thinking compared with rural people who are perceived as old-fashioned, unsophisticated and backward thinking testifies to the prevalence at the C level of discriminatory assumptions that so often go unquestioned (Shucksmith, 2012).

A common dimension of this discrimination is attitudes to accents. Rural accents are often stigmatized, with speakers of such accents often dismissed or marginalized as 'country yokels'.

The way such prejudicial ideas have become culturally normalized means that attempts to justify the discrimination rarely need to be aired. However, when they are, they are generally in terms of 'breeding' taking us back once again to a reliance on pseudo-biology – misperceiving socially constructed distinctions (and thus open to change) as biologically based (and thus fixed and immutable).

The impact of such discrimination can be far reaching – for example, in relation to educational advancement, employment opportunities or roles that are deemed prestigious. And, of course, once again, intersectionality comes into play. These disadvantages will be in addition to other forms of discrimination that can compound one another.

Conclusion

What should now be apparent is that limiting our understanding of racism to the traditional idea of white people discriminating against black people leaves many unacceptable views, assumptions and practices out of the picture. The more holistic picture presented in this chapter should be sufficient to show that racism is far more complex than it may initially seem.

One danger of this broader view of racism is that a hierarchy of discrimination can be assumed by some people. For example, I have come across people who come up with some form of rationale for why one form of racism is more significant or more worthy of attention than others. This is, of course, an over-simplification, as all forms of racism can have deleterious effects ranging from relatively minor to disastrous. For example, a wealthy black man may be able to use his financial and other resources to avoid much of the negative impact of racism, while, say, a Welsh person who is being bullied because they speak a minority language may take their own life as a result of this discrimination. What is needed, then, is not some sort of simplistic league table, but rather an openness to look at racism and other forms of discrimination more reflectively and consider the specific circumstances, rather than overgeneralize. It is to be hoped that this chapter has helped to give a firmer basis of understanding to facilitate such openness.

The extent to which you are likely to encounter any of the various forms of discrimination outlined here will, of course, vary widely depending on geographical location and demographic mix. However, it is safer and wiser to be aware of this broad range of racialized forms of discrimination, partly to be more alert to the issues involved if ever you should come across them and partly to develop a fuller picture of what racism involves and how it works.

The discrimination faced by various groups can often be seen to have evolved from overt hostility to more covert forms of marginalization and exclusion. While there has been progress, it remains essential for us to understand the historical and contemporary dimensions of racism in its various forms. Developing inclusive practice requires ongoing attention to identity, cultural recognition and the lived experiences of minority groups. This includes ensuring that all people subject to racism are visible within equality, diversity and inclusion frameworks, that bias is addressed through reflective supervision and training, and that all people are treated with dignity, respect and cultural sensitivity. West (2025) makes a very apt comment in this regard when he argues that: 'It would be a piss-poor form of anti-racism that only benefited middle-class, able-bodied, heterosexual, cisgender, non-immigrant men of colour' (p. 277).

Exercise 7

What difference does it make to your approach to anti-racism to be aware that the field is broader and more complex than a simple black-white dichotomy?

CHAPTER 8

Religious discrimination

Introduction

A primary feature of religion is a set of moral values. It would therefore be reasonable to assume that religion should have an important role to play in promoting anti-racism. And it is indeed the case that many anti-racist initiatives have their roots in faith communities. However, it is also sadly the case that religion can serve as a basis for discrimination on racial or ethnic grounds.

My aim in this chapter is to show how religious discrimination often overlaps with racism, while also having its own distinctive features. In exploring these issues I hope to highlight the need to focus on the specifics of what can broadly be called racialized discrimination, while also retaining a holistic overview of the wider picture. As Shabi (2024) helpfully comments: 'Racism doesn't translate word for word, pigment for pigment. It targets different minority groups in differing ways, but it echoes as it travels, morphing and adapting to the requirements of those in power' (pp. 29–30).

In this chapter, we examine a range of issues relating to religious discrimination and explore how these relate to racism and anti-racism. We begin with a discussion of sectarianism, focusing mainly on the 'Troubles' in Northern Ireland.

Sectarianism

Later in the chapter we shall explore the significance of discrimination against certain groups of people because of their differing religious background or affiliation. However, we begin with a consideration of discrimination *within* the same religion – that is, between different sects that form part of the same religion, hence the term 'sectarianism'. It is important to consider these issues, as assuming that

DOI: 10.4324/9781003668145-9

religious discrimination occurs only between competing faiths fails to recognize the significance and impact of intra-faith conflict and hostility.

I described earlier how the history of Ireland resulted in a schism between the predominantly Catholic Republic of Ireland and the mixed Catholic/Protestant six counties that remained as part of the UK as Northern Ireland. The situation is highly complex and very sensitive, so has to be approached with caution. But the basic situation is this: what is now Northern Ireland (NI) contains two broad categories of residents, Catholics who have a strong association with the predominantly Catholic Republic (generally referred to as Nationalists) and Protestants who have a strong association with Britain (generally referred to as Unionists). Indeed, many Protestants and Unionists often use the term Ulster when referring to NI, although, somewhat ironically, this contains not six but nine counties – three of which are in the north, but are part of Ireland. The tensions between the two countries therefore have a double edge – partly religious and partly a matter of national identity.

Such tensions peaked during the period of what came to be known euphemistically as the Troubles (late 1960s–1998). Previous tensions had led to segregation – for example, in relation to housing, education and employment, which in turn led to discrimination and an escalation of ill-feeling. The conflict became violent, characterized as a battle between Loyalists (essentially fighting to remain part of Britain) and Republicans (equally fighting for a united Ireland). The deployment of 'peace-keeping' British troops led to a further intensification of ill-feeling and resentment. An already strong desire on the part of Republicans to have a united Ireland without what was seen as British interference grew stronger in response, with the British authorities paying little heed.

Further escalation took the form of Republican terrorist attacks in Britain in an attempt to force the British Government to recognize the claim for a united Ireland. This had the effect of adding to the anti-Irish sentiment and discrimination discussed in Chapter 7. This included Irish communities in Britain being subject to suspicion and surveillance. A strong association between Irish people and terrorism developed (interestingly, making no distinction between Catholic and Protestant).

Yet another escalation arose from the development of Prevention of Terrorism Acts that led to widespread stop-and-search practices, arrests and detentions without trial, with innocent individuals being caught up in this process (Hickman et al., 2005).

Cases such as the wrongful imprisonment of the Birmingham Six and Guildford Four, who were convicted of IRA bombings and later exonerated, highlighted the extent to which Irish people were presumed guilty by association (Greenslade, 2004). This period left a lasting impact on the Irish community, many of whom felt stigmatized and silenced. This meant that the effects of sectarianism were not limited to Ireland.

> **Key point**
>
> The 'Good Friday Agreement' in 1998, which was enshrined in the Northern Ireland Act 1998 saw the establishment of the NI Assembly and devolved government (with a joint First and Deputy First minister from the political majority Unionist and Nationalist parties). The Loyalist and Republican ceasefires that facilitated this, have broadly held, with a corresponding reduction in the level of violence and tension, but it would be a mistake to assume that the underpinning sectarianism has been addressed in either the British or Irish context.

Indeed, as the majority of Irish immigrants to Britain were Catholic and their presence in a predominantly Protestant Britain fuelled sectarian tensions, anti-Catholic prejudice, particularly in places like Glasgow and Liverpool, became intertwined with anti-Irish sentiment (MacRaild, 1999). Irish Catholics were often excluded from social and professional networks, and their religious identity was sometimes perceived as a threat to British national identity, once again highlighting the dual nature of what is commonly referred to as religious discrimination.

But Catholic/Protestant conflict is not the only form of sectarianism. We shall later be discussing Islam and one of the features of this major religion is the split between Sunni and Shia factions – a source of major tensions based on differing interpretations of the same scriptures, particularly in relation to leadership. Sunnis believe that the community should select its leaders (known as caliphs), Shia Muslims opt for leadership remaining within the Prophet's family. As a result of this schism, there are differing practices, rituals and interpretations of Islamic law between the two communities. In the overall scheme of things, the differences between the two sects are not major, but the tensions and conflicts they cause certainly can be.

Anti-semitism

We have already discussed anti-semitism as a form of racism, but it is worth revisiting here, as there is much more to consider if we are to gain a fuller picture and thus be better equipped to address such matters as and when they arise.

Judaism is one of the three Abrahamic religions, alongside Christianity and Islam, so called because they trace their spiritual heritage to Abraham, a key patriarchal figure in their scriptures. The three share in common the belief in one God (monotheism), have prophets as messengers of God, draw on sacred texts (the Torah, the Bible, and the Qur'an) and endorse a set of moral values around justice and compassion.

Despite these commonalities, there are also significant differences and these have formed the basis of major forms of racialized discrimination. As with other forms of discrimination, the oppressive consequences can range from relatively minor to catastrophically major (the Holocaust being a prime example, of course).

The basis of anti-semitism is complex. As Hart (2021) comments:

> Jewishness is more than Judaism. Being Jewish is about having shared culture, heritage and history. Jewish people live, grow and work in many places across the world. There are Jewish communities from Jamaica and Japan, from South Africa. Ethiopia, Nigeria and Morocco, from Poland and Portugal.

> (Dolsten, 2019, p. 77)

What we have, then, is a complex mix of religion (Judaism) and cultural distinctiveness (Jewishness) which overlap, but are not the same. We also have the issue of the Jewish diaspora – that is, the spread of Jews across the world, with local cultures in each case intersecting with both Judaism and Jewishness.

What adds a further complication is the strong association with Israel, the Jewish homeland. This adds a further dimension, that of nationality. As a nation, Israel has come under severe criticism for its treatment of Palestinians, both historically and currently, adding yet another layer of complexity (and sensitivity). Neuberger (2019) makes the important point that: 'criticism of Israel similar to that levelled against any other country cannot be regarded as antisemitic' (p. 40). To assume otherwise would be the equivalent of regarding criticism of American foreign policy as 'anti-Christian'. However, Neuberger qualifies her comment by stating:

> Much of the criticism of Israel does not stem in any way from antisemitism. But, and it's an important but, there is a substantial and growing antisemitic component in the criticism which has been manifesting itself more and more frequently in the spreading of stories that are simply untrue, by ignoring evidence and by drawing conclusions that are wilfully unbalanced.

> (p. 43)

An important practice implication in this regard is the need to ensure that any criticism of Israel does not cross the line into anti-semitism. This is another example of the need for critically reflective practice. Jewishness is much broader than Israel and, even in relation specifically to Israel itself, the basis of its actions towards others cannot be reduced to religion or culture, as that would be a gross oversimplification of some highly complex issues.

TIP! Beware of common stereotypes of Jewish people. These are deeply embedded in popular culture to the point where even committed anti-racists can be taken in by them unless they are alert to their prevalence.

Islamophobia

As I mentioned earlier, Islam is one of the three Abrahamic religions. It has a vast following across the Asia–Pacific region the Middle East and North Africa, Sub-Saharan Africa, with significant Muslim minority communities across Europe, the Americas, Russia and China.

It is based on five pillars:

1. *Shahada* (declaration of faith): This refers to the monotheistic basis of Islam, with Allah seen as the sole God and Muhammed as his prophet or messenger.
2. *Salah* (prayer): Prayer is a key part of Islam, with adherents expected to pray five times a day while facing the Ka'bah in Mecca. This involves specific rituals and recitations based on holy scriptures. Such prayers are intended to show submission to God ('submission' being one of the meanings of 'Islam').
3. *Zakat* (almsgiving): Muslims are expected to donate a small portion of their wealth to support those in need. It is seen as a way of 'purifying' their wealth.
4. *Sawm* (fasting): Ramadan is a month when adherents abstain from food and drink from dawn until sunset. The precise dates vary each year based on lunar cycles. It is intended to promote self-discipline, compassion and spiritual reflection.
5. *Hajj* (pilgrimage): Mecca is regarded as the central point of Islamic worship, and so Muslims are expected to make a pilgrimage there at least once in their life unless they are physically unable to do so or cannot afford to. The Hajj incorporates a set of ritual acts in honour of the prophet Abraham.

Islamophobia literally means fear of Islam, although the term is used more broadly to refer to discrimination against Muslims, whether or not based on fear. It can be seen to operate at all three levels of PCS analysis:

- Personal prejudice, as reflected in discriminatory attitudes, actions and language use.
- Culturally based discriminatory assumptions and stereotypes that both reflect and feed individual prejudices.
- Structural disadvantage in terms of barriers to access to positions of power.

As always, these three levels will interact dynamically, influencing one another, rather than operating in isolation.

Warsi (2024) gives example after example of Islamophobic discrimination, including instances of intersectionality:

> Research published by Bristol University in 2015 shows the extent of discrimination faced by Muslim women, noting that they are 71 per cent more likely than white Christian women to be unemployed, even after controlling

for factors such as language abilities, education, marital status, number of children and strength of religious belief.

(p. 119)

Muslim women can be seen to be especially prone to discrimination on the basis of the perception that they are passive and thus less capable than other women.

There are two important aspects of Islamo*phobia* that need to be considered, specifically in terms of the role of fear. On the one hand, there is the association, fuelled by the media at the C level between Islam and Islamist terrorism. There is a parallel here with how the association between Irish people and terrorism (as discussed in Chapter 7) served to fuel discriminatory attitudes and reactions. The 9/11 attacks in the United States that led to the 'War on Terror' were openly acknowledged to have an Islamist basis. For a significant proportion of the population in the United States and beyond, Islam came to be seen as a faith based on violence, destruction and hatred, even though one of the meanings of the word Islam is peace.

Of course, while the fears and tensions associated with Islamist terrorism are fully understandable and legitimate, one unfortunate consequence of the intensity of feelings has been the blurring of the boundaries between a terroristic minority and the peace-loving majority of Muslims (Shaver *et al.*, 2017). Judging a religion of over a billion people by the actions of an extremist minority is, of course, entirely inappropriate, but none the less quite common in many quarters, clearly fuelled by media outlets that stoke fear by failing to provide balanced representations of Islam.

On the other hand, Islam is also associated with the conspiratorial 'Great Replacement Theory'. This is the view, common in some parts of the United States and elsewhere, that there is a deliberate plan to replace, over time, white people with people from ethnic minorities (Daniels, 2021). Islam is not the only target for this conspiratorial fiction (Hispanic and other groups are included too), but it remains a significant part of the mythology. Once again, irrational fear is at the heart of the problem.

Islamophobia is clearly an example of the overlap of racism and religious discrimination, and therefore makes it an issue that we need to consider carefully, paying attention to the complexities involved.

Discrimination against atheism

There have been times in history when it has been dangerous to declare oneself to be an atheist, and sadly such dangers continue to exist to the present day in some areas. Historically, identifying as an atheist has given rise to significant tensions and challenges particularly in regions with strong religious traditions. While today atheism is becoming more socially acceptable in some areas, the safety of atheists cannot be universally guaranteed.

One of the characteristics of anti-atheistic sentiment and ideology has been persecution, especially in places that operate on a strongly religious basis. Today the situation is that, in some parts of the world, such as the Middle East, atheism can be subject to severe legal consequences to the point of not only imprisonment, but even death (Hariri *et al.*, 2019). In other parts, the costs of being openly atheistic are not so great but can still be significant in terms of social stigma, social exclusion and/or discrimination in the workplace (Gervais *et al.*, 2011; Gervais, 2013).

One feature of discrimination against atheism (and thus atheists) has been the confusion between atheism and anti-theism. The latter involves antagonism towards religion and thus discrimination against people of faith, whatever faith community they may belong to. As such, it is a problematic position to adopt. However, atheism *per se* does not involve being antagonistic or discriminatory towards others on religious grounds. It simply means a choice not to believe in any God or gods. There is nothing inherently anti-religious in adopting a position of atheism. It is perfectly possible – and common – to be an atheist and yet fully respect and support the right of people of faith to have their beliefs and practices without being penalized or undermined for doing so (reflecting a view of 'live and let live').

Interestingly, one example of discrimination against atheism I have come across many times is the denial that such a stance can even exist. The argument goes something like this: You cannot know that there is no God, therefore you cannot be an atheist, you can only be agnostic. The logic of this is, of course, fundamentally flawed. The whole matter is a question of belief. Agnostic, in its literal sense, means 'not knowing', so in a sense everyone is agnostic, even the most fervent believers – no one knows for sure. So, an atheist can be just as fervent in their belief in the non-existence of God as a believer is about His existence. Being agnostic, as used in relation to matters of faith means not knowing whether or not to believe. Atheists and agnostics therefore start from a very different position from one another. Consequently, trying to deny that atheism is even possible as a stance can therefore be seen as a form of discrimination against atheism in itself.

Reflective moment

What role did religion (or the lack of it) play in your upbringing? How has it influenced your views on life in general and religious diversity in particular?

Conclusion

As we have seen, religion or the lack of it can be the basis for discrimination, often on a major scale to the point of killing people on the grounds of their beliefs and associated practices. While religion can be seen to have its benefits, it clearly also has its problems (Thompson and Moss, 2026b). It is not simply a matter of two opposing belief systems challenging each other for dominance; rather, it is much more complex than that, as religions can have internal conflicts (sectarianism) and also overlap with matters of ethnicity and nationality to produce multidimensional foundations for conflict and thus potential discrimination and oppression.

Practitioners and managers do not need to be experts in particular religions, but we do certainly need to be aware of the significance of religion in people's lives and the various ways in which belief systems can clash and thereby produce discrimination.

> **Exercise 8**
>
> What aspects of religious discrimination are you aware of? How might these affect your work or possibly your private life?

CHAPTER 9

Key terms and concepts

Introduction

Choosing any set of concepts to discuss will inevitably lead to questions about why certain other concepts were not included. So, what follows in this chapter is not intended to be definitive or comprehensive, just what I hope will be food for thought and helpful guidance in building on the ideas covered in the earlier chapters.

My intention in offering this chapter is to help you further develop your understanding of the theory base underpinning anti-racism so that you are better equipped to: (i) engage with matters of theory, policy and research relating to race, racism and anti-racism; and (ii) practise in effective anti-racist ways that will enable you to make a positive difference.

The terms are presented in alphabetical order to avoid any assumptions that the order in which they appear represents some sort of hierarchy of importance or relevance. All the terms listed are important (they would not be here if not), but some will be more important than others in certain circumstances. But, in general terms, the point I want to make is that each of these terms has a part to play in developing our understanding and solidifying our effectiveness in practice.

It is a lengthy chapter, so you may want to dip into it from time to time, rather than read it from start to finish. But, however you tackle it, please do make sure you cover each term or concept, as they are all important parts of developing a fuller understanding of anti-racism.

DOI: 10.4324/9781003668145-10

Alienation

Although the fact that this term appears first is just a quirk of using alphabetical order, it is quite appropriate that we should begin with it, as it is such a key aspect of the experience of racism.

This term tends to be used to refer to feelings: feeling as though you do not belong, that you are not welcome or valued. However, on closer inspection, we can see that the emotional dimension is just one aspect of a more holistic phenomenon. It manifests itself in terms of:

- *Other psychological aspects* Alienation can affect our thinking as well as our feelings – for example, it can cause confusion and a lack of clarity in thinking as a result of the negativity involved. It can also affect behaviour. Consider, for example, how much of anti-social behaviour has its roots in disaffection and a sense of disconnect from wider social values.
- *Social* Seeing alienation purely in individual terms is to neglect the wider cultural and structural factors (C and S) and thereby present a distorted picture. One consequence of this can be victim blaming – that is, seeing individuals as responsible for their own alienation as if it is some sort of character flaw or a failure to 'fit in'.
- *Spiritual* Alienation can affect our sense of who we are and how we fit into the world (for example, in terms of self-worth), our sense of purpose and direction and our overall worldview. As such, it can be a significant obstacle to spiritual fulfilment (Thompson and Moss, 2026b).
- *Biological* It could also be argued that there is a biological dimension, in so far as alienation can have an impact on health (Adibifar and Monson, 2020).

Jaeggi (2016) comments specifically on the significance of meaning (or meaninglessness, to be precise). She states that:

> An alienated world presents itself to individuals as insignificant and meaningless, as rigidified or impoverished, as a world that is not one's own, which is to say, a world in which one is not 'at home' and over which one can have no influence.
>
> (p. 3)

She reinforces this point in arguing that:

> Alienation is tied to the problem of a *loss of meaning*; an alienated life is one that has become impoverished or meaningless, but it is a meaninglessness that is intertwined with *powerlessness* and impotence.
>
> (p. 22)

The link with power and powerlessness is, of course, very significant when we consider alienation in relation to racism. It takes little by way of imagination to connect alienation to experiences of racism – indeed, it can be seen that avoiding or resisting feelings of alienation is a major challenge for people subject to racism in whatever form. In fact, it is often a major feat of resilience on the part of people so affected to overcome the negative consequences of racism-related alienation.

In practice terms, what this means is that we all have a part to play in preventing alienation where possible, dispelling it where we can and taking all reasonable steps to support people in their efforts to transcend it.

Allyship

We have already devoted a full chapter to allyship, so my aim here is simply to reiterate its key role as a basis for anti-racism (and, indeed, anti-discriminatory practice in general). We can achieve more by working together in solidarity, whether formally through trade unions, professional associations and/or organized campaigns or more informally by supporting one another in whatever way we can whenever the opportunity arises.

It is important to remember that there are two sides to allyship. On the one hand, it means people who are not subject to racism working alongside those who are in order to achieve anti-racist objectives. On the other hand, it means seeing anti-racism as part of the broader field of social justice, equality, diversity and inclusion and thus being prepared to support one another in addressing the myriad other ways in which people can be discriminated against, demeaned, dehumanized and marginalized.

Alterity

This is a concept introduced by Simone de Beauvoir (2011) in her renowned ground-breaking text, *The Second Sex*. She used it to refer to how the male counts as the standard and therefore the female is non-standard, as in the use of masculine forms of language (he/man) to refer to both sexes ('Every man for himself', 'No man is an island', and so on). Bill Bryson, the renowned travel writer, highlights the significance of this:

> That a subtle and pervasive sexual bias exists in English seems to be unarguable. Consider any number of paired sets of words – *master/mistress, bachelor/spinster, governor/governess, courtier/courtesan* – and you can see in an instant that male words generally denote power and eminence, and that their female counterparts just as generally convey a sense of submissiveness or inconsequence. That many of the conventions of English usage – referring to all humans as *mankind*, using a male pronoun in constructions like 'to each his own' and 'everyone has his own view on the matter' – shows a similar tilt towards the male is also, I think, beyond question.
>
> (1998, pp. 425–6)

The term derives from the Latin word 'alter', which means other, as in 'alternative'. Men are treated as the norm, with women as a deviation from that norm, as 'other' (see the discussion of 'othering' later in this chapter). In linguistic terms, the feminine is 'marked'. This means that the masculine term is taken as the basic form and the feminine as a more specific version relating to women, indicating an implicit hierarchy with men to the fore and women in a secondary position. For example, I once saw a local newspaper headline that stated: 'Woman lorry driver charged with dangerous driving'. If the headline had simply stated 'Lorry driver charged with dangerous driving', it would have been assumed that the driver was a man. 'Woman lorry driver' is the 'marked' term, the one that differs from the norm (which is no doubt part of why the newspaper felt the event was worth highlighting). This is alterity. It can be unproblematic in some circumstances, but quite detrimental in others – for example, when assumptions are made about competence (for example, whether a woman engineer can be expected to be as competent as a man).

Exceptions would apply in areas that are seen as predominantly female domains. For example, the term 'nurse' does not directly indicate a woman, but unless otherwise specified (male nurse), it is generally assumed to refer to a woman. This is one of the ways in which language use (at the C level) subtly but powerfully creates social expectations in relation to gender.

The same logic can be seen to apply to issues relating to race/ethnicity and racism. For example, if the stereotype of a senior leader is a white man, then uncritical acceptance of alterity can create obstacles to advancement for black people – especially women of colour.

Alterity is rarely discussed, but it is deeply embedded within everyday thinking and generally taken for granted. In practical terms, then, this is an example of the 'unlearning' that is needed in anti-racism, the ability and willingness to cast off ideas that were part of our upbringing and our culture.

Anger

I include this term because it has been a topic of conversation on many of my training courses and teaching sessions with students. Exploring it has proven to be very worthwhile. First of all, it needs to be recognized that anger is a legitimate response to racism or indeed any form of discrimination, whether on the part of those directly affected or by allies. However, it can sometimes be misunderstood or assumed to be something it isn't.

From these discussions (and other related experiences), I have become aware of a number of potentially problematic situations:

1. People of colour who have been made to feel that anger is a 'bad' emotion and should therefore not be expressed.
2. White people who have interpreted expressions of anger as hostility.

3. Allies who have been made to feel that they have no right to be angry because they have not been discriminated against.
4. Expressions of legitimate anger that have resulted in disciplinary proceedings or at least threats thereof.
5. The risk of depression arising from 'stifling' anger.

This is not a comprehensive list, but it covers the main issues as I have encountered them. It is worth revisiting each one in a little more detail in order to appreciate their significance.

In terms of 1, the very distinction between 'good' and 'bad' emotions is problematic, as all emotions are potentially helpful or harmful, depending on the circumstances. For example, joy would normally be seen as a positive emotion, but expressing it when being told that someone has died could be highly problematic. It is certainly true that being fixated with experiences that cause anger can give rise to difficulties and can stand in the way of progress in terms of the issues involved. However, allowing negative emotions to 'fester' is also likely to create problems and simply suppressing them is potentially harmful in terms of mental health (see my comments on 5 below).

In terms of 2, equating anger with hostility can lead to defensiveness. Feeling alarmed about anger is an understandable response in certain circumstances, especially if the anger is expressed through raised voices and/or sudden movements. At times, the intensity of emotion can be unsettling, but it should not be a problem if we recognize people's right to be angry about racism and its detrimental consequences.

One danger to be aware of is allowing strong expressions of anger to feed the stereotype that black people are aggressive, prone to violence and therefore not to be trusted.

In relation to 3, interestingly this disavowal of the right of allies to feel angry appears to come more from other allies than from people directly affected by racism. But, wherever the disavowal comes from, it is neither helpful nor justified. I was not abused as a child but having worked in the child protection system as a practitioner, manager and educator over a number of years, I am well aware of the devastating effects of child abuse and the associated trauma, and I feel very angry about it, as I feel I have every right to do. It does not downplay or detract from the anger of children who have been abused (or adults who were abused in childhood). Indeed, it affirms their right to be angry by acknowledging the horrific harm done by abuse (and, in parallel fashion, by racism).

In terms of 4, it can be helpful to distinguish between the expression of legitimate anger and the legitimate expression of anger. While anger about racism is clearly legitimate, this does not mean that all forms of expression of anger are acceptable. One course participant gave an example of someone throwing chairs about in response to a racist comment having been made. While that sort of response is highly likely to be deemed unacceptable and potentially a basis for disciplinary proceedings, it is to be hoped that any managers and HR professionals involved in the situation will be sensitive and supportive in dealing with the matter.

However, there were many examples cited of people facing disciplinary proceedings or being threatened with them for far less extreme expressions of anger. So, it was clearly not simply a matter of how the anger was expressed. We were left wondering to what extent stereotypical assumptions about the threat of aggression or violence were playing a part in these situations (Chavez *et al.*, 2015).

In relation to 5, one theory of depression is that it arises from internalized anger (Kim *et al.*, 2023). It is as if the intense feelings, if not processed, lead to a form of self-defence. This explains why people who struggle with depression can be seen to withdraw into themselves as if they are creating a protective cocoon around themselves. This produces a sort of emotional numbing – if I can't feel it, it can't hurt me. So, in a way, depression – while clearly a problem – can be understood as an attempted solution, a way of trying to avoid emotional and spiritual pain.

One implication of this is that not expressing feelings of anger can increase the risk of mental health problems, especially in relation to depression. We should therefore be very careful not to discourage – deliberately or unwittingly – the expression of anger.

Anger is a common part of a grief response and, when it comes to racism, there are certainly many losses involved. We should therefore find it helpful to think of anger as a manifestation of grief and therefore be prepared to respond with sensitivity, empathy and compassion, even if some strong expressions of anger can be anxiety provoking at times.

It should be clear, then, that we should be very aware of the significance of anger and the dangers of turning it into a problem if we are to play our part in promoting anti-racism.

If you are not used to dealing with people when they are angry, try to make sure that you remain calm and do not panic. This will help to ensure that the situation does not escalate.

Anomie

This is a sociological concept that refers to situations characterized by 'normlessness' – that is, circumstances where we have no established patterns to follow, no sense of what we need to do in response to what we are encountering. An example would be finding ourselves in a setting we have not been in before, not knowing what to expect or what is expected of us (perhaps a new student at university not clear yet as to how it will differ from being at school). It is a very uncomfortable feeling and one that we will seek to avoid or dispel. It has long been recognized that unclear expectations can be a source of stress (Thompson, 2024).

It is something I have encountered when someone meets a person from a different cultural or ethnic background and is unsure of how to relate to them in terms of cultural folkways and norms. This can create tension that can act as a barrier to effective communication and rapport building. While this is not likely to result in direct racial discrimination (racialism), it can produce racist outcomes in the sense that people from a minority culture may be receiving a lower level of service from a human services practitioner or lower level of support from a manager because of this tension and the barriers it can cause. This would not be intentional racism, but it would none the less count as racial discrimination if it means differential levels of service or support based on ethnic/racial factors. Consequently, it is something that we need to be aware of and prepared to guard against.

One practice implication of this concept, then, is that we need to develop the confidence and presence of mind to be able to engage with people from a different culture than our own without any unnecessary tensions or barriers.

In some circumstances, anomie could also potentially play a part in institutionalized forms of racism whereby the unsettling feelings it can generate could lead to the needs of people from minority ethnic groups being deemed to be a lower priority than what their needs and circumstances would suggest. This would, then, not be a simple matter of personal prejudice, but rather a set pattern of response that has become part of an organization's culture and thus institutionalized.

Anti-racism

The point has already been made that anti-racism is an active process of identifying, challenging and changing the values, attitudes, cultural assumptions, structures, behaviours and language use that perpetuate racism in its various forms. I am hoping that, by having reached this point in the manual, you are now aware that anti-racism is:

- *More than non-racism* – avoiding contributing to racism (non-racism) is clearly a good thing, but basically it is not enough. Because racism is a phenomenon that is much more than just personal prejudice (P), we need to be aware of how it is embedded in cultural formations (C) and wider social and political structures (S). If we do not adopt this wider perspective, it is likely at times that we will be unwittingly be reinforcing racist cultural assumptions and structural power relations simply by uncritically being influenced by the wider society that we grew up in.
- *Premised on allyship* – what ten people working alone can achieve is nothing compared to what ten people working together can bring about. Tackling racism is not a challenge solely for people on the receiving end of it. In social justice terms, there is a moral imperative for us all to play a part in developing and sustaining an anti-oppressive alliance.

- *Intersectional* – while some people legitimately prefer to focus mainly on challenging one particular form of oppression (for example, feminists challenging sexism), because different forms of discrimination constantly interact and compound one another, it is important not to lose sight of the bigger picture. So, while focusing *primarily* on one form of discrimination presents no problems, focusing *exclusively* on one certainly does, as it means that other forms of discrimination are not being considered or addressed.

- *Not simply a matter of black and white* – as we have seen, racial discrimination against black and Asian people quite understandably tends to be the main focus of attention, this is not the whole story. What is needed is a recognition that racialized forms of discrimination are many and varied and can be just as oppressive as what is conventionally thought of as racism. A broader perspective on racism can help us to appreciate the need to think carefully about less-recognized forms of racial discrimination without diluting the attention that needs to be given to racism as commonly understood.

- *Complex, sensitive and multidimensional* – unfortunately anti-racist initiatives have often suffered from crude approaches that are *dogmatic* (fixed in their way of thinking and apt to dismiss much-needed debate and analysis as 'intellectualizing') and *reductionist* (prone to reducing complex, multi-level phenomena to simple, single-level explanations). While this dogmatic reductionism continues to be in evidence in some quarters, there has been good progress in developing more sophisticated approaches in others – for example, in terms of professional organizations now taking more interest in racism and anti-racism than was previously the case.

- *Necessary* – it is not an optional extra, it is a central part of good practice in human services, management and leadership, a core component of values-based practice (Thompson and Moss, 2026a). How can managers in any sector who are responsible for the wellbeing of their staff think of themselves as effective leaders if they are allowing racism to go unchallenged in their workplaces and broader society? Likewise, how can human services professionals committed to making a positive difference to the people they serve expect to be successful in their work if anti-racism is not part of their value base?

Authenticity

This is a philosophical term strongly associated with existentialism. It refers to accepting ownership of our choices and associated actions and consequences. It is the opposite of what Sartre (2020) called 'bad faith', by which he meant the tendency to deny responsibility in various ways – for example, making such claims as: 'I can't help it, it's the way I am'; 'It's not in my nature to….' and other such excuses for our actions or inactions.

Sartre sees authenticity as a moral value and not just a technical concept. His view is that, in seeking to see the reasons for our behaviour as being beyond our control, we are trying to absolve the responsibility for our (in)actions and thereby acting immorally. In his later works, he also presented it as a *political* absolution of responsibility and therefore an obstacle to social justice (Sartre, 1973).

In my own work (Thompson, 2025), I have linked the concept of authenticity to leadership by arguing that leaders who do not take ownership of their choices and decisions and, in particular, how these shape the organizational culture are absolving themselves of responsibility and thereby failing in their role as leaders.

The same argument can be put forward in relation to human services professionals. If we seek to wriggle out of our responsibility for dealing with difficult, sensitive and complex issues (as in anti-racism, of course), then we are failing in our duty to promote social justice. Consider the following examples:

- *Unlearning* If we deny that we are able to change ('It's my nature'; 'It's the way I was brought up'), then we will be ill-equipped to reject discriminatory assumptions and stereotypes at the C level that we have been exposed to throughout our lives.
- *Challenging* Anti-racism involves challenging racist comments, actions, policies and systems. If we are not prepared to do this ('I don't have what it takes'; 'I'm too shy, it's my nature'), then again we are failing in our duty to take the necessary steps to make anti-racism a reality. This takes us back to the key principle that, if we are not part of the solution, we are part of the problem.
- *Avoidance* Experience has taught me that many people will avoid sensitive issues like racism. They feel uncomfortable about them, and so they try to navigate their way around them, rather than dealing with them directly. Once again, bad faith can at the root of this problem: 'My parents didn't feel comfortable with these issues, it must be genetic'.

What all these examples show is a reluctance to take ownership for engaging with difficult issues, each one rooted in bad faith or, in other words, a lack of authenticity. We should therefore conclude that authenticity is not simply an abstract philosophical concept, it is an essential practical basis for effective anti-racist practice.

Black

I earlier commented on the difficulties in developing suitable anti-racist language that everyone can agree on. Black is a widely used term in the anti-racist lexicon, but it is not without its difficulties. For one thing, at times it is used in a generic sense to refer to people facing racism based on their skin colour, including Asian people; at other times, it does not include Asian people, as in the acronym BAME (Black, Asian and Minority Ethnic people).

It has its roots in the 'reclaiming of language'. This is a strategy used to counter the discriminatory use of language. For example, 'queer' came to be used as a derogatory term to describe members of the LGBTQ+ community, and so, to neutralize its negativity, members of that community adopted that term to refer to themselves and, in doing so, 'reclaimed it'. In parallel fashion, at one time the polite (but none the less racist) term to refer to black people was 'coloured'. However, the term 'black' came to be used pejoratively (usually accompanied by a directly insulting term). By a process of reclaiming language, it came to be adopted by black people themselves and their allies before coming to be widely accepted as a valid term.

Of course, what complicates matters further is, as we noted in Chapter 7, racism also applies to people who would not come under the umbrella term of 'black'. So, how we use language remains complex and subject to debate (and considerable dispute), leaving us with what I earlier called linguistic sensitivity – that is, critically reflective practice around language use.

Colourblindness

This term refers to the tendency on the part of many people to assume that, if they treat people of colour in exactly the same way as they treat everyone else, they will be engaging in some sort of anti-racist (or at least non-racist) behaviour. It is characterized by such comments as: 'I don't see black or white, I just see people' or 'Skin colour does not matter; we are all the same under the skin'.

Superficially, this sounds like a reasonable position to adopt. However, a more critical perspective helps us to realize that it is a highly problematic approach. Of course, being black or white *should not* make a difference; skin colour *should not* matter, but the colourblind approach fails to take account of the fact that skin colour *does matter*; it has proven to be historically highly significant, to the detriment of people with darker skin tones, and sadly continues to be so. Consequently, colourblindness is an approach that fails to acknowledge the reality of racism, metaphorically brushing it under the carpet, and thereby failing to take account of the way it blights the lives of so many people.

We should therefore make sure that we neither fall foul of this mistaken view ourselves nor allow it to go unchallenged in others where it is acting as a brake on progress.

Colonialism

The word 'colony' comes from the Latin 'colonia' which was used to refer to a Roman outpost. It came to be used to refer to any settlement of a group of people from one country in another land. Colonialism generally refers to how colonies were set up in the development of empires, such as the British Empire. British people settled in various parts of the world, established control and benefited from access to the natural resources in these places and the opportunities for trade they presented.

Implicit (and occasionally explicit) in colonialism was the idea of white supremacy, the myth that the white settlers and the nation they represented were superior to the largely black populations in the areas they settled. There is considerable irony in the fact that part of that sense of superiority was a belief in *moral* superiority. The moral acceptability of not only making ill-informed value judgements about other people, but also shamelessly exploiting their resources was not questioned.

Another sad feature of colonialism was slavery. The people themselves were considered a legitimate resource to exploit, with the forcible removal of enslaved people to other colonies where they would be expected to work on an unpaid basis in terrible conditions. This inhumane practice endured from at least the 14th century to the mid-19th century and, as Sanghera (2021) points out, we are still being influenced by colonialist thinking to this day:

> The legacies of empire run deep and are sometimes contradictory. The pulling down of statues may have created the popular idea that one can erase or retain the values of empire by pulling monuments down or keeping them up, but imperialism exists within us in much more complicated ways.
>
> (p. 107)

Critical race theory (CRT)

This is a term that refers to an intellectual movement and framework concerned with understanding how notions of race and thus associated racist assumptions and practices are embedded in legal systems, policies and sociopolitical structures. In this respect, this manual could be considered an example of CRT in so far as it seeks to go beyond 'commonsense' notions of racism as purely personal prejudice.

Those who would prefer the balance of power in race relations to continue favouring white people appear to see CRT as a threat and are keen to dismiss it by misrepresenting it. For example, West (2025) points out that: 'According to US Senator Ted Cruz, critical race theory says that "every White person is racist" and that "certain children are inherently bad people because of the colour of their skin"' (p. 6) and adds that: 'Badenoch [the Conservative Party Leader] has claimed that critical race theory is an ideology that interprets mere Whiteness as oppression and mere Blackness as victimhood' (p. 7). Once again, we face the problems of oversimplification.

Cultural appropriation

Colonialism involved the exploitation of not only natural resources and of people deemed to be inferior and thus lacking in rights, but also cultural resources – for example, by adopting elements of some forms of art and music, aspects of traditional healing and folk medicine and anything else within the respective cultures, generally without permission, acknowledgement or expressions of gratitude or respect. For example, in some areas in the United States, Native American paraphernalia are sold as tourist merchandise often without acknowledgement or understanding of the culture the items are deemed to represent. I was once in a part of the United States where several shops were selling 'Indian headdresses' as tourist souvenirs and gifts, even though the Native American people in that area did not traditionally use headdresses. So, in this regard, cultural appropriation can be seen as a further reflection of disrespectful colonial exploitation.

This is not to say that there is nothing to be gained from cultures learning from one another, each enriching the other in respectful and empowering ways. But this is very different from cultural appropriation which tends to be one way, unacknowledged and often disrespectful and thus exploitative and disempowering.

Cultural competence

Insensitivity to a person's cultural needs and circumstances is likely to result in racism, in so far as it means that a person from a minority culture receives a lower level of service than a person from the majority ('suffers a detriment', to use the legal term).

Cultural competence therefore refers to the ability and willingness to take account of a person's culture and respond accordingly. To do so effectively involves being aware of our own cultural assumptions and perspectives so that we do not unwittingly impose them on others. This is what Rosenblatt (2016) calls 'humility', being aware of the limitations of the extent to which we can understand another person's perspective and experience. When done properly, cultural competence can be a part of a foundation of anti-racism, but, as we noted earlier, it is not enough on its own.

An important practice implication of this is that we need to be aware of some of the core elements of the culture of any minority communities we work with and be prepared to learn more as and when required. In my education and training work, I have had to reassure very many people that they are not expected to be experts in every culture to be found in their area. However, anyone who is not a Muslim but is working in an area with a certain proportion of Muslims should have at least a basic understanding of its principles and tenets and what these are likely to mean to the people concerned.

Key point

What is also important to note is that we need to talk to people about their lived experience of their culture or religion. Their particular 'take' on their culture may be quite different in some respects from what the textbooks say.

Decolonization

We have come across a number of examples of the harm caused by colonization as part of the exploitative nature of empire building. Decolonization refers to the process of trying to move away from the assumptions and discriminatory thinking that underlies a colonial mentality. It involves identifying and addressing the legacy of colonialism in all its forms in order to ensure, as far as possible, that colonial attitudes, actions, language forms, policies and systems are eradicated from today's organizations and institutions.

An example of this would be the work being done in a number of universities to update curricula to ensure that they are not in any way reflecting or promoting colonialist ideology and its white supremacist basis.

Difference

The literal meaning of to discriminate is to identify a difference (for example, when we discriminate between a red traffic light and a green or amber one). Where discrimination becomes a problem and a source of oppression is when we discriminate *against*. That is, we not only identify a difference, but also use that as a basis for excluding, disadvantaging or ill-treating a person, group or category of people because of a perceived difference.

This, of course, is the basis of racism as well as other forms of discrimination. Racist ideology includes the belief that skin colour, nationality and/or ethnicity are grounds for discriminating against those who are deemed to be 'different' (whether in pseudo-biological, cultural or other such racialized terms).

However, difference does not have to be seen in this way. As the idea of valuing diversity confirms, difference can be a very positive thing, as Figure 9.1 illustrates.

How difference is conceived and used is therefore pivotal in terms of racism and anti-racism. This has clear practice implications, in so far as failing to move away from seeing social differences as a problem or threat will sustain and reinforce discriminatory thinking, while seeing difference as an asset will form a basis for valuing diversity and fostering inclusion.

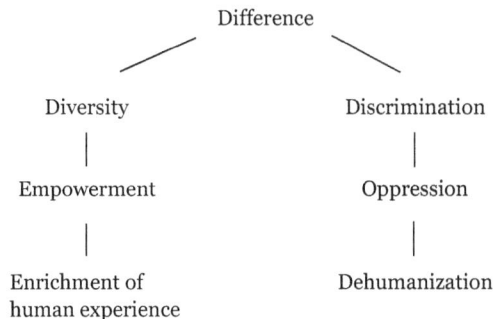

```
                          Difference
                    /                  \
          Diversity                      Discrimination
             |                                 |
        Empowerment                       Oppression
             |                                 |
       Enrichment of                     Dehumanization
       human experience
```

FIGURE 9.1 Difference, diversity and discrimination.

Discrimination

As I have mentioned, to discriminate is literally to identify a difference. However, it is used in a professional, moral-political and legal sense to refer specifically to the process of discriminating against certain people, placing them in a disadvantageous position without legitimate reason.

Such discrimination can be intentional – for example, when someone is deliberately trying to harm, exclude or disadvantage one or more people. Examples would include excluding someone from employment purely on racial grounds, being insulting or derogatory towards members of ethnic minorities and, perhaps the most blatant of all, racist attacks and murders (see the discussion of racialism below). However, what is more common is unintentional discrimination in the form of certain groups of people losing out because of individuals unwittingly relying on discriminatory stereotypes and/or forms of language; the uncritical acceptance of institutionalized policies and practices; biased systems and so on.

An example of the latter would be the growing concerns about racial and gender biases in the training of artificial intelligence engines. It is now clear that such biases have been allowed to feature in the operation of AI in some ways (Coeckelbergh, 2022). It is highly unlikely that the software engineers involved in developing AI were deliberately trying to discriminate unfairly against minority ethnic groups, but the discrimination and its detrimental effects are none the less real.

Discrimination, of course, has major implications for professional practice and management. As I mentioned earlier, such matters have not always been well handled, and so it is essential that we appreciate the complexities, do what we can individually and collectively to address deliberate discrimination and be prepared to identify unwitting discrimination in ourselves and others and make the necessary changes. Discrimination is the process (or set of processes) that gives rise to oppression. Addressing discrimination is therefore a necessary basis for developing anti-oppressive practice.

Diversity

The idea of valuing diversity is based on the recognition that different people have different things to offer and that a lack of diversity can lead to staleness, a lack of creativity and an insular us-them mentality that can exclude people from minority groups.

The variety that diversity brings, by contrast, can stimulate innovation, broaden horizons and foster inclusivity. Diversity enriches us, while the lack of diversity that racism encourages impoverishes and demeans us.

Unfortunately, diversity has been a buzzword for some time now, leading to it being used uncritically and often vaguely. If we are serious about promoting anti-racism and anti-discriminatory practice more broadly, we need to develop a fuller, more sophisticated understanding of diversity and its implications.

The concept of 'valuing' diversity is important. It highlights how appreciating the benefits of cultural and other forms of variety helps us guard against racism which is based on negative perceptions of minority groups. Such negative perceptions can be seen to cluster around two main areas: assumed inferiority and threat. As we have noted, the assumption of inferiority largely has its roots in colonialism. The threat aspect can also be linked to this, as the connection between threat and the 'lower orders' is well established in the popular imagination and thus dominant ideology.

Threat can be seen to apply in two main ways. First, there is the perceived threat of physical violence. Consider, for example, the stereotype of black men as ultra-virile potential aggressors. Media overrepresentations at the C level of black men as violent criminals feed this stereotype. Second, there is the perceived threat of what is often referred to as 'swamping'. This refers to concerns that 'alien' cultures will steadily displace traditional 'home-grown' cultures. For one thing, such concerns are grossly overstated and thus not valid. But, perhaps more importantly, they are misguided.

This is where diversity comes into the picture. There is already considerable evidence of how cultures can merge and blend. Consider the popularity of Indian and Chinese food, the growing interest in 'world music' and other such examples of advantageous cultural connections. But, even without such connections, there is no reason to assume that different cultures cannot live harmoniously alongside one another – unless racist stereotypes get in the way, of course.

Diversity, then, needs to be seen as an important part of anti-racism. When its richness is appreciated, it can play an important part in helping to develop communities and societies based on social justice rather than on discrimination and oppression.

Elegant challenging

Being able and willing to challenge racist views, language, stereotypes, actions, policies and so on is a key part of anti-racism. If such matters are not challenged, it will be assumed that they are acceptable and will continue to proliferate. However, how effective a challenge is depends on how it is done.

There are three basic outcomes from challenging: success in creating change or at least a stimulus towards change: making no impact; or being counterproductive – actually making the situation worse. To get the best results, challenging needs to be *elegant* – that is, tactful and sensitive, not crude or provocative.

If the person being challenged feels that they are being demeaned, threatened or attacked, it is likely that they will not welcome the challenge and will become defensive or even hostile. Elegant challenging, by contrast, involves subtly, gently but firmly questioning the basis of the racist beliefs being evidenced. Examples might include:

- Responding to a racist comment or joke: 'I'm sure you didn't intend any harm, but that kind of comment can come across as offensive. Let's keep our space inclusive and respectful for everyone'.
- This can be contrasted with the following unhelpful comments:
  - 'That was racist—what's wrong with you?'
  - 'You always say inappropriate things'.
  - [Laughter followed by silence or no response at all]
- Responding to a racist stereotype: 'I know that stereotype is pretty widespread, but real-life experiences are much more varied. Actually, I read something recently that challenges that view, so I think we need to be careful about it'.
- As opposed to something like:
  - 'That's such a narrow-minded thing to say'.
  - 'You clearly don't know what you're talking about'.
  - [Rolling eyes or dismissive tone]: 'Seriously?'

Encountering racism can understandably evoke anger, but it is important to stay calm, otherwise you risk the person you are challenging responding to the anger, rather than to the important message you are putting across.

Empowerment

This is another important term that has been plagued by acquiring buzzword status and thus oversimplification. Fundamentally, empowerment is about helping people gain greater control of their lives. This can be understood in terms of PCS analysis:

- *Personal* This includes boosting confidence, helping people move away from self-limiting barriers, facilitating access to resources they need and so on.
- *Cultural* Many stereotypes and culturally based assumptions are disempowering, and so challenging these can enable progress. Helping people break free from restrictive cultural patterns can also be part of this.
- *Structural* Major social divisions, such as class, race/ethnicity and gender empower dominant groups and disempower others, and so working towards changing those social structures (through campaigning, for example) is part of what empowerment is all about.

Empowerment has been recognized as important in the human services as a way of avoiding dependency creation and of promoting the core value of self-determination. In the management field, empowerment of staff is increasingly being recognized as a core element of effective leadership (Huq, 2015). Giving staff greater autonomy boosts confidence, morale and engagement and provides a stronger basis for learning and development.

Reflective moment

Can you think of any examples of situations where someone has empowered you – that is, they have helped you to gain greater control of your life? Is there anything you can learn from these experiences to help you be more effective in empowering others?

Epistemic injustice

Epistemology is the study of knowledge. Epistemic injustice therefore refers to how the knowledge and perspectives of marginalized groups are systematically undervalued or even dismissed altogether. There is a parallel here with cultural appropriation. For example, much of western knowledge believed to stem from the Ancient Greeks can be seen to have its roots in the Arab world, although this is rarely acknowledged (Montefiore, 2021). Similarly, eastern approaches to medicine and healing are often squeezed out by the more dominant western approaches.

Again, we are seeing assumptions of superiority bringing about detrimental consequences. In this way, racist assumptions about what counts as valid knowledge can be seen to be holding back progress in the wider development of knowledge from diverse sources.

Equality

This is a term that has caused a lot of confusion over the years because it has so often been taken literally to mean that we need to treat everybody the same. A more helpful way of looking at it is to think of it as *equal fairness.*

Treating everybody the same involves ignoring people's differing needs and circumstances. Whereas equality, in the sense that it is used in the context of anti-discriminatory practice, refers to treating people fairly, rather than uniformly. In a very real sense, equality relates to the absence of discrimination. As we have noted, discrimination involves using difference as a basis for treating people unfairly, whereas equality involves treating people fairly, despite differences. Diversity then takes us a step further by helping us to appreciate the benefits of social differences and the enhancements they bring – that is, not only moving away from seeing difference as a problem, but also seeing it as the basis for enrichment.

Ethnicity

What differentiates ethnicity from race is its subjective element, in the sense that race is imposed from the outside (people are defined as members of a racial group by others through social construction), whereas ethnicity has a largely self-defining element. This is because ethnicity is about cultural identity, about where we feel we belong and are spiritually 'at home'.

Race tends to be very simplistic as a social construction: them and us, black and white, out group and in group, whereas ethnicity is multi-dimensional. As an example, we can note that many people who objected to Brexit were doing so on the grounds that it went some way towards denying them a sense of European identity, something that added an extra dimension to whatever they saw as their national identity.

A common misunderstanding of the term 'ethnic' as an adjective is that it applies only to minority groups. Comments like 'There are a lot of ethnic people living in that area' show a lack of understanding of ethnicity. *Everyone* has an ethnicity, a cultural background and heritage. But, interestingly, members of majority ethnic groups tend to take their ethnicity for granted, while members of minority ethnic groups normally do not have that luxury as their minority status can be very significant (and very significantly detrimental in terms of racism).

There is a parallel here with linguistic groups. Members of a dominant language like English can afford to take language for granted, while speakers of a minority language often cannot. For example, someone whose first language is not English may be very capable of communicating through the medium of English on a day-to-day basis but may struggle to talk about complex or sensitive emotional issues in English. Consequently, if they were denied the opportunity to, say, receive counselling through their own language, they would encounter challenges and a lower level of service that majority language speakers would not.

Guilt mongering

Looking back historically, there is much to be ashamed of in terms of how minority ethnic groups have been treated; there is no doubt about that. However, there is a difference between recognizing this basis of shame and feeling guilty for actions that we have not been involved in perpetrating. Guilt is an emotion that can give rise to defensiveness and can have a paralysing effect in terms of addressing the issues of concern. This is something I have come across many times in my education and training role, with participants on courses stating that our discussion of the issue had helped them recognize they had a sense of unwarranted guilt that had been making them feel anxious and thus reluctant to participate in anti-racist work.

At one time it was popular to have training courses that openly sought to make white people feel guilty for being white. They were discontinued when it became apparent that they were not only ineffective, but actively counterproductive, in so far as they tended to generate defensiveness and thus a reluctance to engage. It was in the critique of these courses and other such initiatives that the term 'guilt

KEY TERMS AND CONCEPTS

mongering' was introduced to draw attention to the detrimental effects of this ill-advised approach.

A key concept here is that of the 'sins of the father' – that is, the need to recognize the contribution that forebears made to today's racism. If, by this, it is meant that we should be aware of the history of racism and be prepared to address its current manifestations, then it is a helpful concept. However, if it is used to make today's generation feel guilty about what previous generations did, then that is likely to be unhelpful, given the tendency for guilt to block action more often than it motivates it.

Hegemony

This is a sociological term that denotes dominance through ideas. It describes the ways in which power is exercised through language – specific discourses and broader ideologies are said to 'win hearts and minds'. That is, ideas that serve the interests of those in positions of power (the power elite, to use the technical term) are presented subtly and pervasively through social institutions like the media and the education system as being natural and normal and thus beneficial to everyone.

In this way, the process sustains existing power structures and the inequalities associated with them. One example of a hegemonic idea would be the narrative that anyone can achieve success in life if they are prepared to work hard enough. However, it takes no account of how racism creates obstacles that can make any such success a difficult – if not impossible – mountain to climb for people of colour. This idea of 'meritocracy' is presented ideologically as a sound moral principle, but it ignores the fact that racism means that it is not a level playing field. The net result is those people of colour struggle to succeed (however defined) tend to be seen as not trying hard enough or not being capable of success, thereby feeding racist stereotypes.

Another example would be how the legal and criminal justice systems work. People from marginalized communities will often be disadvantaged by a reliance on stereotypes of black people as more prone to criminal behaviour and institutionalized biases that lead to higher rates of imprisonment for minority ethnic offenders (Lammy, 2017). Despite these disparities, the principle of 'law and order' is presented as for the good of all when, in reality, it serves the interests of the wealthy and powerful far more than it serves those of certain other groups, especially people of colour.

These examples highlight how hegemony plays a part in framing systems that are 'loaded' against minority groups as balanced and fair. This has the effect of distracting attention from the inequalities and injustices that the system masks. It is therefore important that practitioners and managers are aware of how these processes work, otherwise we may find ourselves 'blaming the victim' by mistaking systemic disadvantages for personal failings.

> **Key point**
>
> In my experience, the process of 'blaming the victim' (Ryan, 1971) is sadly not uncommon in human services practice or in management. It seems to be based on a failure to see the big picture and appreciate the role of wider factors ('atomism', to use the technical term).

Inequality

This term is used in two senses: (i) in a broad sense as the absence of equality, as defined above (to be treated equally means to be treated in ways that do not involve being discriminated against); and (ii) in a narrower, economic sense as the gap between the richest and the poorest in any given society (Dorling, 2015, 2018).

In the latter sense, the greater the gap between the top and bottom financial levels, the greater the degree of inequality and the greater the prevalence and impact of the social problems associated with inequality (Wilkinson and Pickett, 2011), especially around mental health (Wilkinson and Pickett, 2018).

Byrne (2024) highlights the significance of inequality in the following terms:

> Not so long ago ... Barack Obama, called inequality the 'defining challenge of our time'. He was right. Inequality – the market that creates it, and the politics that permit it – slows our commerce, threatens our climate, incites conflict, excites corruption, and has created, in the UK, not a sceptered isle of proud dignity but the indignity of a realm where the luckiest live like princes and the poorest live on charity.
>
> (p. 2)

Byrne then goes on to link together economic and other forms of inequality in stating that: 'From Plato to Aristotle and beyond – to Aquinas, Hegel, Hobbes, Locke, Hume, Kant, Marx and Mill – there has long been a recognition that inequality of wealth underpins all other inequalities' (p. 5).

Of course, racism contributes significantly to inequality in both senses of the word. In relation to the former, we have already noted many ways in which racism deprives certain groups or categories of people of fair and equitable treatment. In relation to the latter, racism can be seen to not only contribute to people of colour being overrepresented in the poverty statistics in the first place, but also erect barriers in terms of being able to get out of the poverty trap (obstacles to high-quality education, discrimination in employment, higher rates of illness and so on).

Inequality, some people have argued, is necessary because if we were all the same, there would be no motivation to better ourselves. For one thing, this view makes the mistake of interpreting equality to mean sameness (rather than equal fairness), and for another it fails to recognize the immense hardship, suffering and lost opportunities inequality brings.

Inclusion

One of the consequences of racism is the large-scale systematic exclusion of people from ethnic minorities from positions of power. In line with our earlier discussions, we should note that such exclusion is not necessarily deliberate, but it does serve the interests of people in positions of power to disregard such inclusion, if they even notice it at all.

Institutionalized discrimination is a major source of exclusion. Consequently, efforts to promote inclusion (integration initiatives in schools, for example) can therefore be understood as reactions against such institutionalized discrimination.

The concept of inclusion is closely associated with the disability rights movement. It is premised on the way in which even kind-hearted compassionate people can create problems for disabled people by not recognizing how their actions (or inactions) and the systems they are part of serve to exclude people with disabilities.

Institutional racism

This term is often used in a commonsensical way to mean racism perpetrated by organizations (that is, institutions). However, it has its roots in sociology where it refers to racist processes that are *institutionalized* – that is, so well built in to policies, procedures, processes, practices and systems that it largely goes unnoticed most of the time. Discrimination becomes the default setting – that is, it will tend to happen unless steps are taken to prevent it.

Institutional racism can be found in various aspects of public life: people of colour often receive harsher punishments in the criminal justice system; a higher likelihood of being stopped and searched by the police; lower levels of funding for schools located in areas with higher than average students from minority ethnic groups; and racial inequalities in the quality of healthcare. West (2025) captures the situation well when he states that:

> No anecdote, or collection of anecdotes, no matter how shocking, or captivating, or terrible, can scientifically prove that people of colour are treated worse than White people in schools, in hospitals, in public spaces, at stores, or by the police. Data is what we'd need to make statements about the prevalence of racism in all these areas of life: rigorous, empirical data.
>
> Fortunately, data is precisely what we have.
>
> (p. 37)

Likewise, Rutherford (2021) reinforces the idea that, although at one time, (misguided) science contributed to racist views, its findings are now clear in establishing the various ways in which racial discrimination is embedded in so many aspects of social life (that is, institutionalized).

The significance of institutionalized racism is another reason why we need to look beyond the individual if we are to develop a more adequate understanding of racism (and other forms of discrimination), hence the emphasis in this manual on PCS analysis.

Intersectionality

Chapter 5 was dedicated to exploring and establishing the importance of intersectionality and it is worth revisiting here.

There are specific features of the experience of racism that need to be carefully considered, just as there are distinctive elements of sexism, ageism, disablism and so on. It is therefore important that each area of discrimination is studied closely and addressed in its own right. However, there is also a need to understand how these different areas act as what I have previously called 'dimensions of experience' or 'multiple oppressions' (Thompson, 2021). This refers to the need to understand people holistically, with all these dimensions considered as a whole, not each one in isolation. As we noted earlier, a black woman will experience both racism and sexism. To this we must add other forms of discrimination around age, disability, religion, language group, sexuality and so on.

As humans, we are complex, multidimensional beings. To be understood fully, each of those dimensions needs to be taken into account, but so too must the overall picture of how they relate to one another and 'intersect' (hence the term). Intersectionality therefore requires us to think holistically and thereby forms the basis of the 'anti-oppressive alliance' we discussed earlier.

Microaggressions

This refers to the various subtle ways that racist assumptions manifest themselves. An example would be a black person regularly being asked where they are from, as if it is being automatically assumed that being black means being a foreigner. Another instance would be a Muslim or Hindu being asked what their Christian name is when required to fill in a form.

Barack Obama, in an autobiography, refers to having been watched or followed by staff when browsing in shops (Obama, 2020). Other examples would include a black person in a senior position being assumed to be in a junior position; countering affirmation of Black Lives Matter with the dismissive 'all lives matter' (thereby totally missing the point); and expecting people of colour to be experts in racial discrimination (parallel with expecting all women to be feminists).

The prefix 'micro' is significant, in so far as each incident can be relatively minor in its own right, but when they occur consistently and persistently, their cumulative effect can be quite devastating, steadily feeding a sense of alienation and eroding confidence and self-worth.

Microaggressions are generally not intended to cause offence or create difficulties, but they are none the less problematic. As I explained earlier, it is not the intention that counts, it is the outcome. Racist outcomes do not cease to be racist just because they are based on ignorance and/or insensitivity.

From a practice point of view, we therefore need to ensure that we ourselves are not involved in perpetrating or perpetuating microaggressions while also being prepared to elegantly challenge any instances that are proving problematic and educate people about these issues where appropriate.

Oppression

In my *Anti-discriminatory Practice* book (Thompson, 2021), I define oppression as:

> Inhumane or degrading treatment of individuals or groups; hardship and injustice brought about by the dominance of one group over another; the negative and demeaning exercise of power. It often involves disregarding the rights of an individual or group and is thus a denial of citizenship. Oppression arises as a result of unfair discrimination – that is, the disadvantages experienced as a result of discrimination have oppressive consequences.
>
> (p. 50)

This is a major part of the reason why we need to pay attention to discrimination in its various forms. Oppression is clearly antithetical to health and wellbeing, learning and development and spiritual fulfilment, and so, at all times, we need to ensure that we are taking the necessary steps to tackle all forms of harmful discrimination, including, of course, racism.

Othering

In relation to racism, this refers to seeing white people's experiences as normal and natural and therefore to see black people's experiences as a deviation from that, as 'other'. There is a parallel here with alterity, as discussed above.

There is also a link with alienation, with othering being a significant source of feeling alienated. People of colour will often be seen and portrayed as foreign, exotic and strange, different from the norm, rather than just a variation on the human norm. Othering therefore easily evolves into alienation and a sense of not belonging.

Othering, as a concept, needs to be understood in the context of intersectionality, in so far as people can be subject to othering in a number of (interacting) ways:

- Kulvinder is the only Asian member of the team at work and also the only disabled member. She often feels like an outsider in terms of both her ethnicity and her disability. Her specific perspective or needs are generally ignored. At first, she takes it personally and her confidence suffers because of it. However, she gradually starts to realize that there is a process of othering going on.

- Duwayne is the only black regular at his local pub and is much older than the others. Nobody is openly hostile to him, but he often feels uncomfortable and wishes there was another pub nearby where he could feel more at home. He had opportunities to be among older people at the local day centre, but he would be the only black person there or he could spend time volunteering at the local youth club where he would be among a number of black people, but would be by far the oldest person there.

- Miriam is one of only two women on the board of the charity she supports. The two most dominant voices on the board are strongly Christian men who speak often speak openly about 'doing Christ's work' and tend to pay little attention to women's issues. She had hoped to get support from the other woman on the board to incorporate more emphasis on women's perspectives, but she was rebuffed, suspecting that her colleague did not feel comfortable about collaborating with a Jewish woman.

Othering is therefore a potentially highly destructive and problematic process. However, it is not inevitable. It is perfectly possible for people to welcome and incorporate people who are in a social minority in ways that avoid feelings of not belonging. What basically contributes to othering is a failure of inclusion based on a related failure to value diversity.

Reflective moment

Have you ever been treated as 'other', as if you don't fit in because you are deemed to be 'different' in some way? If so, what range of feelings did the experience give rise to? If you have never experienced it, what would you anticipate it would be like?

Passing

People subject to certain types of discrimination can, at times, avoid being discriminated against by concealing whatever it is about them that could give rise to negative treatment. For example, an Irish person who is victimized at work as a result of anti-Irish sentiment may be able to avoid discrimination in the wider community by not letting it be known that they are Irish. This is what is known as passing, they could 'pass for' being, for example, English.

However, in other forms of discrimination, passing is not always possible – for example, discrimination based on skin colour or tone. For example, a white gay man in a pub where a drunken man is aggressively expressing homophobic and racist comments may be able to avoid being attacked by 'passing for' straight, but a black man in the same circumstances is unlikely to be able to 'pass' for white.

This is an important consideration when it comes to risk assessment, in the sense that opportunities to avoid harm will differ depending on the extent to which passing is an option.

A further aspect relates to people from a minority ethnic group whose skin tone is such that it creates ambivalence in terms of perceived racial grouping. In such circumstances, the individuals concerned can decide to pass as white to gain the associated privileges of being part of the dominant group or to identify as black in keeping with their family background and ethnic heritage. Those that choose to opt for the privileges can, however, face a backlash from members of their community who feel betrayed.

It is also important in terms of identity and self-esteem. Someone forced to pass for their own safety may feel very uncomfortable about having had to do so, as if they are somehow betraying their identity and heritage. Similarly, anyone who chooses to pass – to gain social or career advantage, for example – may feel guilty about doing so.

Postcolonialism

The British Empire played a key role in the development of colonialism – that is, the process of invading other countries, dispossessing the people to be found there of their rights and, importantly, their material resources (land, minerals and so on) and relegating them to second-class status.

As so much of the colonialism took place in Africa and Asia, there was a demarcation between colonizers and colonized in terms of skin colour, with the latter being deemed inferior and even subhuman. This, tragically, was the basis of the development of the slave trade.

The term 'postcolonialism' is used to refer to the current era in which such enslaving activities are deemed to no longer take place, but where the consequences of the brutal history remain with us in terms of racist attitudes, actions and language use. That is, while the practices of colonialism appear to no longer occur, the ideology that was used to justify the cruelty, inhumanity and oppression are still to be found in many places.

Power

This is a central concept, in so far as it underpins so many of the other concepts commented on here and indeed so much of what the book is all about. In particular, it relates strongly to PCS analysis, as all three levels, P, C and S, involve the use of power (Thompson, 2007).

Power takes many forms and operates in many ways. As the work of Foucault (1980) has helped us to understand, power can be used positively or negatively. In terms of its negative use, in my own work (Thompson, 2018c), I have distinguished between the deliberate *abuse* of power (as in racialism) and the unintentional *misuse* of power (for example, when someone relies on a racist stereotype without realizing the harm they are doing). Both are unacceptable, of course, but the response to each needs to be different.

In a sense, both anti-racism and anti-discriminatory practice more broadly can be seen as a reclaiming of power, making positive use of power to challenge its negative uses, what is often referred to as 'speaking truth to power'. So much power comes from people working together, which is why we need an anti-oppressive alliance, rather than in-fighting or point scoring.

> **TIP!** Beware of the common mistake of assuming that power is necessarily a bad thing. Yes, it often does harm when it is abused or misused, but it is also a source of considerable benefit in a number of ways.

Prejudice

This term refers literally to prejudging – that is, making our mind up about someone or something in advance. As such, it involves making assumptions about people. Technically, it can be either positive or negative. A positive prejudice could amount to being overoptimistic about a person. For example, having been highly impressed by students from a particular university, you may prejudge that all students from that university are highly capable, only to be disappointed when you eventually learn that your prejudice was not well founded.

Of course, when it comes to anti-racism, it is *negative* prejudices that we are mainly concerned with. A core element of racism is a set of unfair and inaccurate negative prejudices about people of colour. Prejudice is therefore an important concept when it comes to promoting anti-racism and our efforts must include avoiding any prejudices of our own, as well as elegantly challenging them in others and, where appropriate, educating people about them.

However, we need to avoid overemphasizing the significance of prejudice as a factor in racism. Once again, we need to return to PCS analysis to appreciate that prejudices (at the P level) are only one set of factors, with close attention being paid to the wider cultural (the C level being the source of many prejudices anyway) and structural context. Focusing predominantly or exclusively on prejudice will mean that we are leaving very important issues out of the picture and thereby operating on the basis of a very narrow and distorted picture that can be problematic in practice.

Privilege

This is another term that can cause confusion. A privilege is a benefit a person enjoys that is not a right afforded to everyone. Some privileges have to be earned, while others are given simply by virtue of who the person is or what group or category they belong to.

The notion of 'white privilege' refers to benefits that accrue to white people simply because they are white (a certain degree of respect and trust, for example) that are not necessarily afforded to people of colour. Not being continually stopped and searched by the police would be an example of white privilege – something that I, as a white person, can take for granted that many people of colour (especially young males in urban areas) cannot. As Eddo-Lodge (2018) puts it:

> Neutral is white. The default is white. Because we are born into an already written script that tells us that to expect from strangers due to their skin colour, accents and social status, the whole of humanity is coded as white. Blackness, however, is considered the 'other' and therefore to be suspected.
>
> (p. 85)

This is also relevant to the earlier discussions of alterity and othering.

It could be argued that privilege is not the right concept, in the sense that the key issue is not the privileges that white people (and other dominant groups) have, but rather the lack of rights that people of colour (and other marginalized groups) are denied. Returning to my example above, not being stopped and searched unnecessarily by the police should be seen as a right applying to everyone, rather than a privilege for white people. One person's privilege is very often another person's right denied. None the less, discussion of privilege can be productive and helpful in highlighting racial disparities.

Privilege is also a term that needs to be used sensitively, as privilege is a relative matter. I recall a training course where one of the participants related how she had talked with a female student she was supervising on placement about white privilege, only for the student to become quite angry and distressed. The student pointed out that she had lived in dire poverty, had been sexually abused as a child, relentlessly bullied for having a speech impediment, survived an abusive marriage and had two miscarriages with her current partner. And now, she said, you are telling me I am privileged! Of course, being white in a racist society does bring certain privileges, but such matters need to be seen as a part of a broader context of life experience and handled sensitively.

Another important point about privilege is what you do with it. Being privileged is not necessarily a bad thing, but using it to put down other people, for example, clearly is. Privilege can at times be used positively – for example, men supporting anti-sexist initiatives or white people supporting anti-racism in a spirit of allyship.

Racialism
As I mentioned earlier, racialism is a form of racism characterized by deliberate racist acts, overt racist attitudes and commonly support for right-wing extremist

views. In effect, it is a form of fascism rooted in the false belief that certain racial or ethnic groups are superior to others and are therefore entitled to additional rights, privileges and benefits. In its most extreme form, it denies the right of certain groups or categories of people to exist, as happened in Nazi Germany in relation to the Holocaust.

It is important to distinguish between racialism and other forms of racism. This is because so often people will claim not to be racist when (i) they are certainly not racist; but (ii) they do not appreciate that they may be unintentionally being racist by relying on stereotypes, uncritically implementing racist policies and so on. That is, they lack an understanding of institutionalized or systemic racism and their unwitting part in it. The result will often be defensiveness, as they assume that they are being accused of being racialist, rather than understanding that racism broadly defined is often unintentional (that is, misguided rather than malicious or evil).

Drawing a parallel with sexism might prove helpful in clarifying racialism. Men will often behave in ways that are gender biased by relying on sexist stereotypes, failing to consider women's perspectives, uncritically implementing sexist policies and so on without at any point wishing to discriminate against women. It is problematic behaviour but it is not necessarily intentional. Contrast this with out-and-out chauvinism where certain men look down on women, have no respect for them, knowingly treat them as second-class citizens and so on. The latter is the equivalent of racialism.

The distinction between racialism and racism more broadly is very significant in terms of how we should respond to the problems created. Where the actions are based on malice (racialism and chauvinism), a disciplinary or legalistic response is likely to be what is needed, whereas discrimination based on naivety, insensitivity or lack of understanding is best served by awareness raising and education. Where people have experienced suitable awareness raising and education but persist in problematic behaviour, then that can be grounds for switching from a supportive educational one to one based on sanctions.

Racialization

As we have noted, race is a socially constructed (and therefore relatively arbitrary) category and not a biological one. Racialization is therefore the term used to refer to how certain groups of people can come to be viewed through a racial lens. For example, Jewish identity derived originally from Judaism, a religion. However, it has come to be racialized, in the sense that Jews tend to be regarded, in terms of the dominant ideology, as members of a *racial*, as well as a religious, group.

Similarly, in biological terms, there are no significant differences between white Eastern Europeans and white British people, but the process of racialization has come to define the former as a different racial entity.

This process is highly significant as it will often serve as the basis of racial discrimination, in so far as it not only creates (socially constructed) differences, but also establishes a racial hierarchy, a sort of in-group vs. out-group relationship, with potentially very detrimental consequences for the latter group of people.

Restorative justice

This is an approach to addressing injustices, whether they arise through criminal activity or discrimination and oppression. It focuses on repairing harm and addressing the underlying causes of such harm, generally through constructive dialogue and reconciliation.

It is now widely used as part of the criminal justice system where perpetrators are called upon to take steps to repair the harm done by their actions or compensate for them in some way. However, there is great potential for similar methods to be used in situations where individuals, groups or communities have suffered harm as a result of discrimination, including racial discrimination – for example, by promoting a culture of understanding and support within communities. As such, restorative justice offers an approach that facilitates dialogue, accountability and a reworking of existing power structures to promote social justice.

Stereotype

A stereotype is a fixed, oversimplified misleading representation of a group or category of people. The use of stereotypes is a basic part of discrimination in general and racism in particular. They play a central role at the C level in representing certain people in discriminatory ways. As such, they are very powerful as they influence people without their being aware of it for the most part. Indeed, stereotypes are so deeply embedded in cultural assumptions that they will generally go unnoticed until someone points them out.

They become a core element of people's view of the world in general and of certain people in particular. They are often used in discriminatory humour and are widely disseminated by the media. For example, in watching a movie, a television drama or reading a popular newspaper, you do not have to wait long before encountering one or more stereotypes of some kind.

Stereotypes need to be understood in the context of intersectionality. For example, a black older woman may be subject to racist, ageist and sexist stereotypes in ways that produce complex discriminatory power dynamics that can be profoundly disempowering.

Clearly, then, our anti-racist endeavours need to steer clear of stereotypes and challenge them whenever we encounter them. Some people may use stereotypes deliberately to demean an individual or group, but for the most part, they will be used unwittingly. But, as I emphasized earlier, it is outcomes that count, not intentions, so we need to recognize that stereotypes are harmful even where no harm or disrespect was intended.

Structural racism

PCS analysis helps us to realize that there is more to racism than simply personal prejudice. The existence across society of social divisions, such as race/ethnicity, class, gender, language group and so on creates a *structural* framework, an intersecting network of social factors. So, when people use the term structural racism or structural discrimination, they are focusing on how problems arise not so much at the level of individual prejudice, but rather in terms of the power dynamics at this higher and broader level of sociopolitical structure.

PCS analysis also teaches us that the three levels, personal, cultural and structural interact with one another in complex ways. So, to recap, the P level is embedded within the C level, in the sense that our personal views and perspectives do not operate in a vacuum – the personal level is heavily influenced by cultural factors; in turn, the cultural level is embedded within the structural level in so far as the dominant ideas at the cultural level tend to reflect (and reinforce) the interests of the dominant groups at the structural level. For example, racist attitudes at a personal level will owe much to racist assumptions and stereotypes at the cultural level (through the media and humour, for example) and these cultural influences (discourses and ideologies) do not operate in a vacuum either; they stem from the structural level in service of the interests of dominant groups (predominantly affluent white men). See the discussion above of hegemony, which forms part of this process.

Suffocated grief

Doka (1989) made an important and highly influential contribution to the literature on loss and grief when he introduced the concept of 'disenfranchised grief', by which he meant grief that is not fully recognized or socially sanctioned, leading to grieving people's needs often not being acknowledged, addressed or met. Examples would include people grieving a suicide loss (stigma), children's grief ('They're too young to understand') or grief experienced by older people ('They get used to it'). Disenfranchised grief can therefore be understood as a significant problem when it comes to people needing grief support.

Bordere (2017) has taken this logic a step further by highlighting the significance of what she calls 'suffocated grief', a concept that is very relevant to anti-racism. The term refers to when people not only experience grief that goes unrecognized, but also encounter discriminatory reactions that compound their distress and vulnerability. Examples would include:

- Young people of colour expressing their grief through crime or anti-social behaviour being treated in a punitive, rather than supportive and empathic way (Livings *et al.*, 2022).
- In higher education, ill-conceived bereavement policies may lead to grieving students facing punitive measures due to rigid attendance and performance policies that fail to account for their grief (Thomas-Jackson *et al.*, 2025).

■ Some traditional cultural expressions of grief may be disregarded or even penalized, potentially leading to a profound sense of deprivation and alienation in their grieving process (Wood and McMahon, 2024).

Clearly, anti-racist practice needs to be aware of suffocated grief and be prepared to prevent it where possible and address it where it does arise.

Systemic oppression

In Chapter 5, we discussed the importance of systems as a basis for understanding the complex processes that give rise to racism (and, indeed, other forms of oppression). The term 'systemic oppression' is used to refer to the processes of discrimination that are not directly linked to personal prejudice, but rather to the institutionalized patterns that are built in to both organizational and wider social systems. In this regard, systemic oppression is closely related to institutional discrimination.

A fundamental implication of systemic oppression is that, if we are to make anti-racism a reality, then we need to address the systems aspects and be able to think in systems terms (Ison and Straw, 2020) – that is, be able to think holistically and not reduce everything to the individual level. Systems do not have a mind of their own, but they do have a logic of their own, in the sense that they operate independently of individual actions. For example, cultures can be understood as systems. A team culture could remain operative over a number of years, even though, during that time, there has been a complete change of personnel.

Being able to 'tune in' to cultures and other systems is therefore an important building block of developing anti-racism.

Unconscious bias

This is a term that has achieved buzzword status in recent years. It denotes the various ways in which racism (and other forms of discrimination) are perpetuated unwittingly as a result of unintentional bias that largely goes unquestioned. Stereotypes would be a good example of this. As I mentioned earlier, for the most part, people relying on stereotypes do not realize that they are doing so – they are just acting and thinking in line with what they were taught as part of their upbringing (through the influence of the C level).

In my view, the term is a mixed blessing. On the one hand, it helps to highlight the need for us all to look critically at the assumptions we make and take on board the fact that you do not have to be a committed racialist to be contributing to racism. As I have emphasized, it is outcomes that count, not intentions. On the other hand, it is problematic, as it focuses attention on the P level and has little to say about where such biases come from in terms of the C and S levels. In this regard, it is a backward step. It is ironic that Prince Harry has spoken out about unconscious bias but, as a member of the Royal Family that spearheaded colonialism, he seems to have little to say about the wider foundations of racism.

In addition, West (2025) highlights the limitations of this concept in stating that:

> It is a mistake to look at the mountains of evidence for discrimination in employment, in healthcare, in policing, in the service industry and in many other areas and attribute it entirely to unconscious bias. Indeed, the scientific research has never even demonstrated that most contemporary bias is unconscious, only that some of it is unconscious. In many instances, the people being racist are perfectly aware of what they're doing.
>
> They're just trying not to get caught.
>
> And very often they succeed.
>
> (pp. 90–1)

What could be labelled 'unconscious bias' is certainly part of the picture, but it is clearly not the whole story. Racism, as we have seen, can be either deliberate or unintentional, but either way, it raises concerns that need to be addressed holistically and not simply at the level of the individual.

Whataboutery

This is a term generally used to dismiss or play down concerns about racism. It is characterized by such comments as: 'You talk about racism, but what about white people, they get discriminated against too?' or 'You go on about anti-semitism, but other religions get discriminated against too'. What we have here, then, is yet another example of the oversimplification of complex issues. It may well be that white people get discriminated against in some cases, but that in no way justifies racism or makes concerns of racism any less valid. Likewise, the fact that any religion can face discrimination does not mean that religious discrimination is any less unacceptable.

Whataboutery tends to arise in situations where there is some degree of reluctance on one or more persons' part to face up to the reality of racism. This reluctance may be due to underlying racist views that they want to keep hidden or it may simply be that they lack awareness and don't feel comfortable talking about complex issues that they do not understand. Either way, it is a potential obstacle to progress and therefore something we need to be aware of and be prepared to address in whatever reasonable way we can.

White

I have already commented on the difficulties of settling on terminology that works for everyone. I have also mentioned how the complexities of how language works have also created tensions and misunderstandings at times. The term 'white', when referring to people, fits right into that picture.

It is generally used to refer to the ethnic majority in terms of skin colour, although in global terms, dark-skinned people are in the majority in numerical terms (but not in power terms). This is the first complication. The second is that people come in a broad range of skin tones, and so any white/non-white binary is largely arbitrary, even though in sociopolitical terms, whether you are defined as white or black can have major implications in terms of status, level of safety and acceptance, education and employment opportunities and other life chances.

Of course, both white and black are social constructions and do not reflect any major biological differences. Consequently, both terms are 'loaded', in the sense that they bring with them different political implications and connotations in different circumstances and how they are used by different people. While it is not by any means a taboo word, we do need to be aware that it is not as straightforward as it might initially appear and we therefore need to use it cautiously.

Some people write it with a capital W to show that it is a social construct and not a literal description of skin colour. But, however we write or say it, we have to be aware of its association with a sense of white superiority (see the discussion below of white supremacy), just as black is often associated with negatives (black day, black mark against you, and so on).

White fragility

This term, associated with the work of DiAngelo (2019), describes the discomfort and defensiveness displayed by many white people when issues around racism are raised. In my education and training experience, I have seen two sides to this. On the one hand, I have had some course participants having tears in their eyes in recounting how they had previously attended courses where they had experienced hostility and had been made to feel that they were evil people – a reflection of what was known as race awareness training. This was an approach to addressing racism that soon became discredited because its confrontational approach proved counterproductive. It was clear that some people had actually been traumatized by such experiences. Interestingly, the trainers adopting this misguided approach were often white.

The other side of white fragility is also something I have come across a great deal in my work. I have had occasion to have a quiet word with a course participant who seemed ill-at-ease and reluctant to join in discussion. Each time what would emerge would be an acknowledgement that they had never thought about racism before and the recognition that they may have contributed to it, albeit unwittingly, made them feel extremely uncomfortable. It would take them a while to come to terms with that recognition, but bringing it out into the open seemed to prove cathartic (they were often the people who were most effusive in their positive feedback at the end of the course).

No doubt there would be people on such occasions who were harbouring racist views and were careful enough not to make them known, but it is to be hoped that exploring the issues could at least have begun a process of rethinking problematic views.

It is important to recognize that the reluctance to engage with anti-racism that white fragility represents helps to sustain racism by foreclosing conversations about the issues and thereby reinforcing the unequal status quo. DiAngelo argues for the need for white people to engage in critically reflective practice and be involved in difficult uncomfortable conversations about race, racism and anti-racism.

Clearly, not all white fragility can be put down to hostile, demeaning styles of training. Consequently, in terms of practice, we need to be able to recognize white fragility as a potential problem and explore ways of addressing it sensitively and constructively.

Key point

Racism and anti-racism are, as I have indicated, complex and sensitive issues. This means that we need to be prepared to discuss the issues openly, to be constructive and to support one another, rather than be defensive or attack one another.

White supremacy

A system of power that privileges white people and reinforces racial hierarchies through social, political, and economic structures.

Xenophobia

This term describes a fear of strangers. There is a parallel here with concepts like Islamophobia and homophobia, where the literal meaning of phobia is fear, but much more is encompassed in how these terms are used. They strongly imply not only fear of, but also discrimination towards the people so labelled.

Once again, we come to the twin factors of a sense of superiority and feelings of threat, with foreigners being perceived as lesser beings and potentially disruptive and/or aggressive. In a sense, xenophobia is the opposite of valuing diversity. This partly explains why so many people are against immigration, even when it can be a benefit to the country (filling labour shortages, contributing to the economy through consumer purchases and paying taxes, cultural enrichment and so on).

While xenophobia as a fear response operates at the P level, it is very much fed by the media at the C level, with anti-immigrant sentiment and jingoism being rife, thereby preserving the power base of the elite at the structural level.

What is also significant about xenophobia is that it is so often extended beyond its literal meaning. For example, xenophobic attitudes can lead to hostile attitudes towards people of colour who can be seen as 'foreigners' even if they, their parents and even their grandparents were born in this country. Xenophobia can therefore be seen as part of racism, and so challenging it needs to be part of anti-racism.

Conclusion

On more than one occasion in this book I have warned against the dangers of oversimplification, and so, in bringing this chapter to a close, I want to emphasize strongly that the terms and concepts here have simply been touched upon, the tip of the iceberg, as it were. The chapter is intended to give you some degree of clarity and to get you thinking about the issues. It is certainly not intended as anything even approaching a definitive guide to the concepts covered. I therefore very much hope that what this chapter will have done is to encourage you to find out more, to explore further and not make the mistake of assuming that you now know all that you need to know about each of these important terms. Once again, I refer you to the *Guide to further learning.*

Racism and anti-racism are sensitive matters, which means that many people are reluctant to engage with the issues in anything more than a superficial way. This can lead them to want a simple, straightforward way of handling situations involving race, ethnicity and related matters. But, as we have seen, the oversimplifications that arise from this are highly problematic.

Consequently, we need a much more sophisticated understanding of what is involved so that we are much better equipped to not only understand racism and anti-racism, but also to play an important role in challenging racism and other forms of discrimination. In this way, then, theoretical concepts can be seen to have an important role to play in providing a foundation for developing that fuller understanding and thereby informing more adequate efforts to make effective anti-racism a reality.

Exercise 9

Which three terms from the ones covered in this chapter have struck you as the most significant? In what way(s)? What difference might they make to your approach to anti-racism?

CHAPTER 10

Pitfalls to avoid

Introduction

In many of the training courses I have run over the years around discrimination and oppression, I have included a session around pitfalls to avoid. In every case, this would generate extensive discussion, highlighting considerable anxiety about such matters. In view of this, I felt it would be helpful to include a chapter here on a selection of such common but potentially very harmful pitfalls. I cover ten in total, beginning with the 'Four Fs' and then moving on to the 'Six Ds'.

Please do note that this is just a selection and is not intended as an exhaustive list.

The Four Fs

Fear

Instilling fear in people is not generally an effective way of bringing about a change in behaviour, attitudes or values – in fact, it will often lead to entrenchment. Unfortunately, though, some people in the past have adopted a hectoring, hostile, accusatory approach to promoting anti-racism, as if their aim is to make people feel guilty, rather than to help them to learn and change. While the legitimate expression of anger about racism can be cathartic and therefore helpful, the deliberate use of generating fear in an attempt to bring about change is likely to be counterproductive and encourage defensiveness. The irony here is that, if we are not careful, attempts to tackle oppression can be oppressive and demeaning in their own right. This takes us back to the need for elegant challenging.

DOI: 10.4324/9781003668145-11

Fragmentation

By this I mean the tendency, thankfully less common than it used to be, for pro-ponents of different campaigns against discrimination and oppression to operate in isolation and not pay attention to common threads. Here are just some of the real examples I have come across in my own personal experience:

- The gay rights activist who happily disparaged older people as 'wrinklies'.
- The disability rights campaigner who wanted to exclude Romani and Travel-lers from the anti-racist agenda.
- The feminist who dismissed promoting the Welsh language and culture as a waste of money.
- The anti-racist tutor who described same-sex relationships as 'disgusting'.

If we are to have a genuine and effective anti-oppressive alliance, then we need to get considerably better at thinking holistically about discrimination and oppres-sion, listen to one another's concerns and support each other in moving forward. This does not stop us from focusing on a particular area of interest and concern, such as anti-racism, but it does help us to locate such areas in the broader context of efforts to promote social justice.

Following fashion

I have been involved in efforts to promote social justice for over 40 years and, during that time, I have seen various fads and fashions come and go – for exam-ple, in relation to the use of terminology. The danger here, as I see it, is that people can lose sight of the important issues by being sidetracked by a concern with what is the 'new' way of doing things (even though what is often presented as new is an old idea rebadged). An example of how following fashion can be a pitfall was captured by someone in a consultancy project I was involved with who said to me: 'We are not focusing on equality now; we are adopting the diver-sity approach' – clearly oblivious to the fact that valuing diversity is a key part of promoting equality.

Forgetting

The world of work tends to be highly pressurized these days, often too pressur-ized (Jaffe, 2021). One of the consequences of this is that people often adopt a 'heads down, get on with it' approach to their work and focus narrowly on the tasks in hand. This can mean that they lose sight of wider issues, lose touch with their values and therefore slip unintentionally into ways of working and think-ing that are not consistent with anti-racist practice. In effect, they forget how important these issues are because they are so narrowly focused on deadlines and keeping their heads above water in coping with a huge workload. While this is understandable, it is also very dangerous.

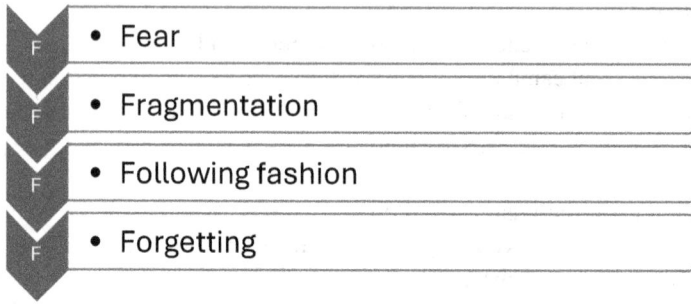

Figure 10.1 The Four Fs.

The Six Ds
Dogmatism
I see this as being related to anxiety. Concerns to avoid criticism create tension; tension contributes to rigid thinking; and rigid thinking leads to dogmatism. By dogmatism, what I mean is the unhelpful view that there is one right way to go about anti-racism and no room for alternative perspectives or approaches. This is clearly unsatisfactory not only from an intellectual point of view (by discouraging critical thinking), but also from a practice point of view, as it serves as an obstacle to the development of innovative approaches to rising to the challenges involved.

Disregarding the complexities
This is a theme I have emphasized a number of times. This is because, over many years, I have regularly come across oversimplified approaches that risk doing more harm than good. The complexities arise from the various strands of the historical context that have led to today's situation, the intricate interplay across different forms of discrimination, the constantly shifting social and economic circumstances and various other factors as well. We therefore need to be wary of simple answers and focus instead on using critical thinking to make sense of how best to move forward.

Doing the bare minimum
This will often arise from defensiveness (the less I engage with anti-racism, the less risk I run of being criticized for my efforts), but it can also be a reflection of complacency. In addition, it can manifest itself as tokenism, by which I mean just doing enough to make it look as though the issues are being taken seriously. For example, I have come across a number of teams who have anti-oppressive practice as a standing item on their team meeting agenda, but when I have asked whether that produces meaningful discussion and action, I have generally encountered a stony silence.

Defensiveness
This takes us back to the first of the four Fs, fear. Being accused of being racist is, of course, what most if not all people want to avoid. It is therefore understandable

that people will be cautious, but unfortunately that caution will often be taken to more extreme limits and manifest itself as defensiveness. 'Covering your back' becomes the order of the day, which means that no real anti-racist steps are being taken, learning is being blocked and the detrimental effects of discrimination are being allowed to continue unchecked. Caution is one thing, defensiveness quite another.

Defeatism

In my experience, this can apply at two levels, general and specific. At the general level, the challenges brought about by neoliberalism of excessive pressures and inadequate resources can easily produce a culture of low morale that saps motivation and feeds a defeatist attitude. At the specific level, feeling overwhelmed by the challenges of anti-racism in a context of the prevalence of ingrained attitudes and a lack of political will at governmental levels can also lead to defeatism as a form of 'compassion fatigue'. While making progress is not easy, defeatism virtually guarantees that progress will not be made.

Doing people down

Regrettably, the culture of the academic world tends to be a competitive one. The 'currency' is prestige – this is what attracts the best staff and students and helps to get research and other funding. Competing for status therefore becomes the norm, with the result that so much of the academic literature is about doing other people down by highlighting perceived flaws. A focus on what different thinkers have in common and how useful collaborations can develop tends to take a back-seat far too often, a tendency that inhibits progress. Thankfully, there are many exceptions where groups of committed scholars have worked together to make a positive contribution to theory and/or practice by swimming against the tide of the dominant competitive culture. This focus on 'doing people down', rather than focusing on common ground, is not limited to the academic world, but it does tend to be more common there because of that status-based culture.

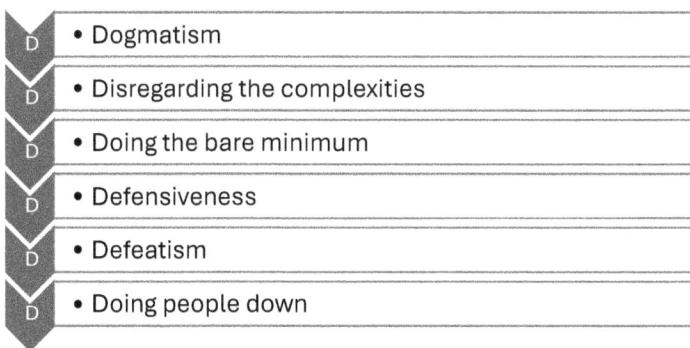

D	• Dogmatism
D	• Disregarding the complexities
D	• Doing the bare minimum
D	• Defensiveness
D	• Defeatism
D	• Doing people down

Figure 10.2 The Six Ds.

Conclusion

There is no guarantee that being aware of these pitfalls will ensure that you never fall victim to them but, on the basis that 'forewarned is forearmed', I am hopeful that the discussions here will prove of benefit.

I am also hopeful that, if ever you do have problems because of one or more of these pitfalls, you will take the opportunity to learn from the experience so that you are better prepared next time a similar situation arises.

We need to make sure that the sensitivities associated with racism and anti-racism do not produce a defensive response that leads people to brush mistakes under the carpet and pretend they did not happen. A more honest approach in which we acknowledge mistakes and learn from them is much wiser and likely to be much more effective.

Exercise 10

Which of these pitfalls are you most likely to be prone to? How can you make sure that you avoid them?

CHAPTER 11

Practising anti-racism

Introduction

The word 'practice' is highly significant. While I have necessarily drawn on theory as an essential underpinning of forms of practice that do justice to the complexities involved, the main focus of the book is on *practice* – that is, making a positive difference in real-life situations, whether in our professional roles or in our lives more broadly.

Consequently, my aim in this chapter is to present what I see as some of the key elements of effective practice. Again, I have to mention that, in a short introductory book, it would not be realistic to attempt to offer a comprehensive analysis. But, I am confident that what I do offer will be a helpful step in the right direction.

I am structuring my ideas around the theme of *discovery*, a process of finding ways and means of playing an important role in making sure that we are all, regardless of our own ethnicity, class or other social position, part of the solution and not part of the problem.

The DISCOVER framework

What follows, then, is a set of eight guidelines that spell out DISCOVER, serving as what I hope will be a useful mnemonic.

■ **D**evelop your knowledge, skills and confidence. I have emphasized how complex the issues are and how dangerous oversimplification can be. It is therefore essential that we continue to develop not only our knowledge and

DOI: 10.4324/9781003668145-12

skills, but also our confidence. There will always be new issues to consider and work on.

- *Include issues of ethnicity and identity.* This applies across the board, but it is especially applicable to assessment work. For example, in my role as an expert witness, I have had sight of very many case records where such matters were paid little or no attention, even though they could well have been highly significant. Ethnic identity is a key part of spirituality (our sense of who we are, how we fit into the world, our sense of purpose and direction and so on), the neglect of which can be a significant disservice to the people we are trying to support empower and/or protect (Skelton, 2017).

- *Support one another.* We will be far more effective if we support one another as part of an anti-oppressive alliance. No one can do what anti-racism requires alone, but we can each play a part and the more we do this collectively, the more powerful and effective our efforts are likely to be. This means putting aside any other differences (competing for status, for example) and developing solidarity. This can be on a micro level, such as in teams, or at more of a macro level, such as through professional organizations and trade unions.

- *Consider the impact of racism on people's lives.* If you have not been directly on the receiving end of racism yourself, there is a danger that you will be complacent about such matters. If you have experienced racism, you are more likely to be tuned in to its immense significance for others. However, I remember a black participant on one of my courses telling me that, in the early days of her professional experience, she had found her own feelings too 'raw' and painful and had therefore found herself glossing over such issues in other people's lives. It was only, she said, some excellent supervision from a black manager that helped her to get past this.

- *Overcome anxiety.* It is important to deal with anxiety calmly and effectively and not allow the sensitivities and high stakes involved in anti-racism to foster defensiveness and a lack of confidence. Such defensiveness creates a 'walking on eggshells' mentality that creates unnecessary tensions and barriers and stands in the way of learning and the development of creative approaches.

- *Value the learning.* However experienced, knowledgeable and competent we are, it is still highly likely that we will get things wrong from time to time. That can be painful, but it can also be productive, in the sense that it can help us learn and grow and be better equipped for the next time a similar situation arises. So, whether things go well or go awry, the potential for learning is something we would do well to capitalize on.

- *Elegantly challenge.* 'Confronting without being confrontational' is another way of describing what this is all about. Challenging in ways that

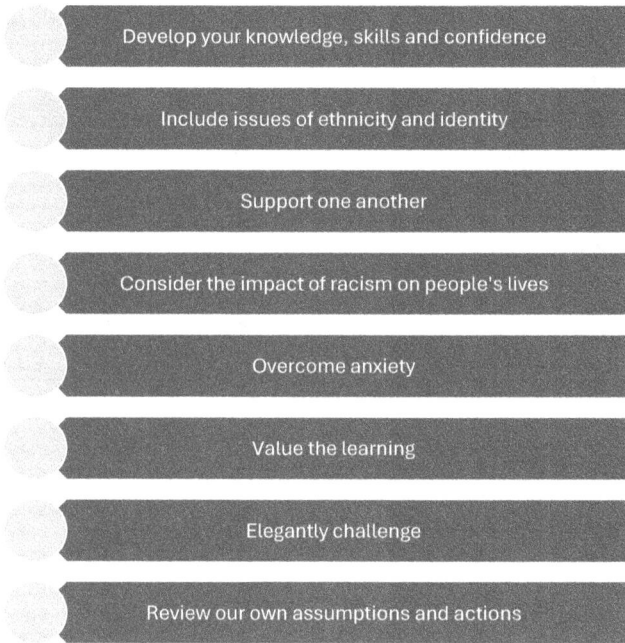

Develop your knowledge, skills and confidence

Include issues of ethnicity and identity

Support one another

Consider the impact of racism on people's lives

Overcome anxiety

Value the learning

Elegantly challenge

Review our own assumptions and actions

FIGURE 11.1 The DISCOVER framework.

cause people to lose face is likely to be far less effective than doing so in sensitive, supportive and empowering ways. Provoking a defensive reaction is counterproductive, and so we need to make sure that any challenges we make are constructive and well targeted and not seen as an attack. We should note that this applies to challenging polices and cultures as well as challenging individual actions, attitudes or language use.

■ R*eview our own assumptions and actions.* An important part of reflective practice is 'reflexivity', the ability and willingness to review our own role in situations (Thompson and Thompson, 2023). Each of us has our own 'lenses' through which we view the world, and those lenses will often reflect our cultural background (the C of PCS analysis). As we know, such cultural backgrounds will often contain discriminatory assumptions and stereotypes that we need to 'unlearn' if we are to optimize our anti-racist efforts. Reviewing our assumptions and our actions is therefore an important basis for reflexivity.

Conclusion

Anti-racist practice is difficult, demanding and fraught with all sorts of pitfalls for everyone concerned. But, if we are able to: (i) recognize the fundamental importance of rising to these challenges for the sake of both the quality of professional practice and social justice more broadly; and (ii) work together in a spirit of solidarity and shared endeavour, then we can make a real difference and know that we are part of the solution, not part of the problem.

The DISCOVER framework is not by any means comprehensive or exhaustive, but as I said earlier, it should help to move us forward positively.

Exercise 11

Look again at each of the eight elements of the DISCOVER framework and consider what you can do to play your part in making progress.

---

126   CHAPTER 11

CHAPTER 12

What next?

Introduction

Now that you have made your way this far in the book, with the end in sight, we come to the question of 'What next?'. Given that this is a book for people at various stages in their anti-racism journey, where do you need to go next in order to go beyond beginner level? The answer to that question is going to be different for different people, depending on their circumstances. However, it is likely that there will be common themes. I have combined what I see as some of the main themes into another mnemonic, structured around the word BREATHE, on the basis that breathing is what enables us to survive and also gives us the opportunity to flourish.

Making sure we BREATHE

Be aware

These are vitally important issues, so it is essential that we are 'tuned in' to what is at stake and what steps we need to take to play our part. And we all have a part to play.

Read

We are fortunate to have a large and growing literature around racism and anti-racism as well as around related areas of discrimination and oppression. I am hoping that this book will have been very informative for you, but please do see it as the beginning or the next step of your reading and not as the end of it.

DOI: 10.4324/9781003668145-13

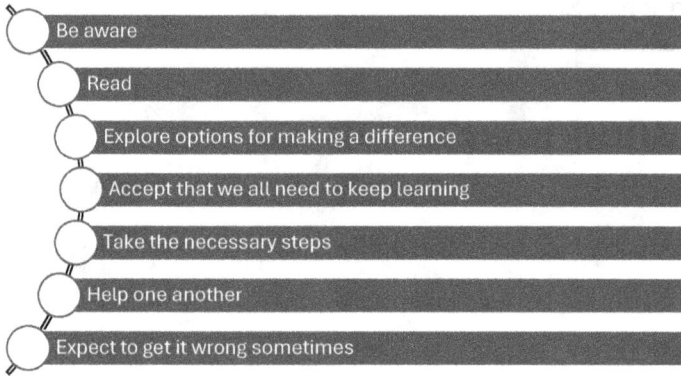

FIGURE 12.1 BREATHE.

Explore options for making a difference
There are so many ways in which we can challenge racism and promote anti-racism. The more creative and innovative you can be, the more options there will be to make a positive difference.

Accept that we all need to keep learning
I have been studying, practising, teaching and writing about anti-racism for decades, but there is still much for me to learn. When it comes to learning about such complex and important matters, there is no 'endgame'.

Take the necessary steps
Don't let anxiety, defensiveness or fear of making mistakes stop you from doing whatever you need to do to make a positive contribution to anti-racism.

Help one another
The more we work together, the more power we have and the more effective we can be. The more solidarity we can develop, the more we can make an anti-oppressive alliance a reality.

Expect to get it wrong sometimes
Given the complexity of how racism operates in society and the different strands of anti-racist efforts, it should come as no surprise to learn that even the most committed, knowledgeable, skilful and competent individual will get things wrong from time to time. We just need to apologize where appropriate, learn from the experience and move on. This, of course, is exactly what Chapter 11 was all about.

Conclusion
I hope that the book as a whole will have spurred you on to learn more and do more, and that this chapter in particular will have given you a clear and helpful framework to guide you.

It should be very clear by now that there are no easy answers to the challenges presented by the prevalence of racism, but there are things we can all do to move in the right direction, steps that we can take that have the potential to make a positive difference.

The BREATHE framework is certainly not the only way to tackle racism but it can help to provide a clear basis for moving forward.

Exercise 12

Are there any aspects of the BREATHE framework you feel you might struggle with? If so, what can you do about it? Who is the best person to help and support you?

CHAPTER 13

If

Introduction

In my *Anti-discriminatory Practice* book, I refer to the political slogan: if you are not part of the solution, you must be part of the problem (Thompson, 2021). This reflects the need for a fully anti-racist approach, not one that complacently settles for so-called non-racism. In this chapter, I want to explain some of the main ways in which people may indeed be part of the problem, rather than part of the solution. So, in a way, this short chapter is a way for you to make sure, and fully satisfy yourself, that you are indeed part of the solution.

Are you part of the solution?

- If you are a student and you are reading this book simply to get a quote or two for an essay, you are not part of the solution.
- If you are a practitioner or manager reading this book in a spirit of defensiveness, wanting to avoid being accused of racism, you are not part of the solution.
- If you are a white manager supervising black staff and simply want to manage your own anxiety about doing so, you are not part of the solution.
- If you are an academic reading this book as part of plan for boosting your career standing, you are not part of the solution.
- If you believe that reading one short introductory book without engaging with the wider literature or seeking to make sure that you use your learning to improve your practice, you are not part of the solution.

However, if you are prepared to keep building up your knowledge base, keep developing your skills base and shore up your value base in a genuine spirit of

DOI: 10.4324/9781003668145-14

wanting to make anti-racism a reality, then you are very likely to be part of the solution.

As I mentioned earlier, a saying we don't hear very often these days, but which used to be quite common, is: 'Racism is a white person's problem'. Of course, this did not mean that white people suffered more from racism than black or other minority ethnic groups did. It meant two things:

1. White people have a moral responsibility for playing a part in tackling the immensely destructive consequences of racism; it is not enough to leave the struggle to the people on the receiving end of the discrimination and oppression; and
2. Everyone – black, white or of any ethnicity – is demeaned by a social system that allows such unacceptable practices to continue to wreak so much significant damage to so many people's lives.

Conclusion

Racism undermines our common humanity, destroys dignity and impoverishes us all – especially, of course, those who are on the receiving end of its destructiveness. Different people will have different motivations for wanting to learn about racism and anti-racism, but if a genuine desire to challenge (and ultimately eradicate) racism is not the primary rationale for doing so, then we need to question the ethics of being associated with anti-racist endeavours.

Exercise 13

How do you make sure that you are indeed part of the solution and not part of the problem? What might hold you back from making progress?

Conclusion

Many years ago, I attended an evening class on philosophy. The tutor was not only very knowledgeable, but also very skilful in putting complex ideas across very effectively. One thing he said in one of the lessons has stayed with me. He argued that no one has ever seen a chair. This seemed to be a strange thing to say, given that we were in a room that had about 30 chairs in it. It turned out, though, that he was making a valid point. He went on to say that, when we look at a chair, we see only one aspect of it – front, back, side or whatever. No one sees the whole chair; we have to mentally construct the rest of it.

He was using this very effective teaching technique to introduce the importance of phenomenology, a philosophical approach that emphasizes the importance of perception and helps us to understand that we all see the world through our own 'lenses'. My perspective on the world may be very different from yours for various reasons. One person's perspective may be very similar to others, but they will never be identical. This is part of what makes each of us unique.

Society has a part to play in this too. This is because what each person sees through their unique 'lenses' will pass through social 'filters', things like culture, class, ethnicity, gender and so on. So, the fact that I am Welsh, from a working-class background, heterosexual and so on will play a significant part in who I am and how I see the world.

As a white person, I see the world from a point of view of relative privilege, having not had to contend with the many disadvantages of skin colour that a racist society imposes on so many other people. However, as a Welsh person, I am used to having my language and culture mocked and dismissed as an irrelevance and to be treated as a sort of second-class citizen in an anglocentric world. Mild

DOI: 10.4324/9781003668145-15

by comparison with the experience of so many people of colour, of course, but very significant and detrimental, none the less.

Sadly, a history of colonialism and slavery has created a set of social filters that lead to far too many people seeing the world through a lens that gives them a sense of superiority because of the colour of their skin, their nationality, their class, the language they speak or their religion, or any combination of these.

Power relations of dominance/subordination at a structural level (S) feed (and feed off), a culture of racial inequality (C) that then shapes actions, attitudes and language use at the personal level (P). These power relations and the associated cultural assumptions and norms then create a scenario of institutionalized discrimination – that is, forms of discrimination, including racism, become firmly established in systems, processes and practices, with the result that the overt racism (or racialism) of the minority is augmented by the unintentional racism of the majority who largely remain unaware of the consequences of the assumptions they are making, the stereotypes they are relying on and the problematic language they are using.

There are no easy answers to these very significant challenges, but there are things we can do, steps we can all take to move in the right direction. My hope is that this book can play at least a small part in raising awareness and spurring a desire to find out more and do more. Individually and collectively, we betray our humanity if we allow racism to continue without doing the best we can in difficult circumstances to reduce it and ultimately eradicate it. We need to work together constructively, as Shabi (2024) so aptly puts it:

> It seems to me that one of our responsibilities is to generate a language and analysis that are neither led by nor replicate the noxiously divisive, racial-hierarchy-producing contours of our mainstream political conversation on such issues. Only then might we gain a deeper understanding of how different kinds of racism operate, how each still impacts on society today. Only then might we forge a compassionate, powerful and unshakeable understanding of our joint struggle. As antiracists all in it together.
>
> (p. 96)

Epilogue

This book forms part of the Routledge *Practice Manuals for Busy People* series, alongside *Values-based Practice* (Thompson and Moss, 2026a). Both manuals highlight the significance of such core values as equality, diversity, inclusion, social justice and dignity. I see these as fundamental to best practice across the human services and in management and leadership across all sectors.

Putting values into practice is not a straightforward matter; it raises all sorts of complications and dilemmas that necessitate an approach rooted in critically reflective practice. We have to be prepared to think carefully about the issues involved and be honest and brave enough to question our own assumptions. Also, where necessary, we need to unlearn the discriminatory lessons we were taught in our upbringing as part of the process of socialization into a culture and society that is based on power dynamics that often suit the power elite more than people in general.

Being involved in anti-racism is not easy, but it is vitally important. There are no simple formula approaches that you can develop, no mechanistic methods to adopt. It involves both head and heart – both intellectual engagement with some very complex issues and an emotional – and even spiritual – commitment to addressing injustice, cruelty and oppression based on arbitrary differences.

It is to be hoped that this manual will have helped you rise to these challenges and leave you better equipped to play your part in making progress towards a more just and empowering society. It is a lifelong journey, so reading this manual should certainly not be the end, but rather another step on the way, and one you can return to from time to time, partly as a reminder and partly to recharge your batteries.

This last point is particularly important, as there will inevitable be times when you start to flag, when the enormity of the task starts to get you down, when you

DOI: 10.4324/9781003668145-16

need some time out from the struggle (self-care is part of anti-racism too). But, if we work together, we can support each other through the difficulties as well as celebrate the successes we achieve, knowing that tackling discrimination and oppression, whether racism or other forms of injustice is worth the effort.

The manual has presented you with a great deal of theoretical knowledge, not for out its own sake but, in keeping with the rationale behind the *Practice Manuals for Busy Professionals* series, as a basis for well-informed, safe and effective practice that can really make a positive difference.

In line with my teaching, training and published work, I have emphasized the need to think holistically and see the big picture, thereby avoiding the common mistake of focusing too narrowly on the individual level. Yes, psychology is very important, but sociology and the other social sciences also have a part to play in forming an adequate foundation of understanding to guide practice.

Part of that big picture is the importance of intersectionality. Over the years I have seen too many people splinter off into silos, focusing on one form of discrimination and neglecting others, thereby failing to see how they connect together or to recognize the common processes and factors that apply across them. Thinking in intersectional terms is an essential basis for the anti-oppressive alliance we need if we are to not only achieve the best results but also create the support systems we need to support, guide, nurture and empower one another in facing the struggles involved. As a good friend of mine once put it, hang together or be hanged alone.

Afterword

The importance of race in shaping our societies remains as urgent and complex today as ever. Since the first edition of this book, the discourse around racism and anti-racism has not only deepened but also become more contested. We are witnessing a fierce backlash against efforts to create more inclusive and equitable systems – a weaponization of terms like 'woke' and an increasing tendency to dismiss anti-racist work as ideological rather than necessary. In this environment, the second edition of *Anti-racist Practice* could not be more timely or more needed.

As a diversity, equity and inclusion (DEI) practitioner and lawyer, I continue to observe how the language of racism – institutional, structural, systemic – is often co-opted, misunderstood or diluted. This book remains a rare and refreshing resource because it dares to engage with that complexity, while offering both clarity and practical guidance. The expansion of the text to include deeper theoretical tools, such as PCS analysis, the DISCOVER framework, and dedicated chapters on intersectionality and allyship, equips readers not just to understand racism, but also to act meaningfully against it.

What remains unchanged is the core challenge: we must move beyond non-racism and commit to anti-racism. As I shared in the first edition, being non-racist allows us to sleep easy while injustices persist around us. Being anti-racist demands more – it is a conscious, daily decision to make equitable choices, even when they are uncomfortable. That choice must operate at all levels: individual, interpersonal, institutional and systemic.

This second edition goes further in unpacking how racism is not merely a matter of intention but of impact – and how deeply embedded cultural and structural forces sustain inequalities. It reinforces the message that anti-racism is not a destination but a lifelong process of learning, unlearning, listening and acting. It invites us to engage with humility, to expect discomfort and to treat mistakes as opportunities for growth – not as reasons to retreat.

What gives me hope is that this book also foregrounds collective responsibility. The chapter on allyship reminds us that anti-racism is not the burden of the oppressed alone. We must reject the tendency to 'dump' the responsibility for change onto those most harmed. Instead, we must build anti-oppressive alliances, standing shoulder to shoulder in the pursuit of justice.

In his book *How to Be an Antiracist,* Dr Ibram X. Kendi writes: *'To be anti-racist is a radical choice in the face of history, requiring a radical reorientation of our consciousness'*. Indeed, choosing to be anti-racist is a moral stance – a commitment not only to justice, but also to humanity. Racism is, at its core, a moral failing. Anti-racism, then, must be understood not just as activism or compliance, but as moral courage.

Thank you for engaging with this work. I hope that in reading this second edition, you have found renewed understanding, greater confidence and a stronger commitment to action. Let this not be the end of your journey, but the beginning of a lifelong, principled practice.

Let us not be passive observers of injustice. Let us be participants in change.

Garth O. Dallas MBA, LLM, FRSA
Co-Founder, Director, Dallas Consulting
https://dallasconsulting.co.uk

Guide to further learning

Developing and sustaining anti-racist practice is a lifelong journey requiring continuous learning, critical reflection and engagement with a variety perspectives. This guide has been developed to help you take your learning further, bearing in mind that this manual is just a short introductory overview and certainly not all you need to know. It is divided into three parts:

■ Part one presents my own work.
■ Part two offers selected books, journals, and contributions from other key authors.
■ Part three highlights online resources and training and professional development opportunities.

Whether you are a practitioner, student, manager or leader, these resources are intended to support your commitment to anti-racism anti-discriminatory practice more broadly.

Part one: My own work

The following books present key ideas developed over decades of work on discrimination, oppression and social justice.

Thompson, N. (2017a) *Social Problems and Social Justice*, London, Bloomsbury. Explores the connections between social problems and injustice.

Thompson, N. (2018a) *Applied Sociology*, New York, Routledge.
Emphasizes a sociological approach to understanding oppression and inequality.

Thompson, N. (2018b) *Effective Communication,* 3rd edn, London, Bloomsbury.
Examines the relationship between language and discrimination.

Thompson, N. (2018c) *Promoting Equality: Working with Diversity and Difference,* 4th edn, London, Bloomsbury.
A more advanced follow-up to my *Anti-Discriminatory Practice* book.

Thompson, N. (2019) *Promoting Equality, Valuing Diversity: A Learning and Development Manual*, 2nd edn, Brighton, Pavilion.
A training manual for tutors, trainers, and managers.

Thompson, N. (2021) *Anti-Discriminatory Practice: Equality, Diversity and Social Justice*, 7th edn, London, Bloomsbury.
Introduces PCS analysis and has been widely used across the people professions.

Thompson, N. and Cox, G. R. (2025) *Age and Dignity: Anti-ageist Theory and Practice*, Cheltenham, Edward Elgar.
Argues the case for including anti-ageism in our anti-discriminatory efforts.

Thompson, N. and Moss, B. (2026a) *Values-Based Practice*, 2nd edn, London, Routledge.
Offers practical guidance on integrating values into practice.

Part two: Broader literature and research
This section brings together influential and diverse sources across disciplines, offering foundational knowledge, lived experience, and critical theory.

Books on race, racism and anti-racism

Ahmed, S. (2012) *On Being Included: Racism and Diversity in Institutional Life*, Durham, NC, Duke University Press.
A critique of symbolic diversity efforts in institutions.

Baddiel, D. (2021) *Jews Don't Count*, London, TLS Books.
Highlights the neglect of antisemitism within broader anti-racism discourses.

DiAngelo, R. (2019) *White Fragility: Why It's So Hard for White People to Talk about Racism*, London, Penguin.
Introduces the concept of white defensiveness and its systemic implications.

Eddo-Lodge, R. (2018) *Why I'm No Longer Talking to White People about Race*, London, Bloomsbury.
A passionate call for awareness of the insidious and persistent nature of racism.

Griffiths, J. (2021) *Speak Not: Empire, Identity and the Politics of Language*, London, Zed.
An important discussion of the politics of language.

Hooks, b. (1996) *Killing Rage: Ending Racism*, New York, Holt.
A thought-provoking exploration of racism and anger,

Kendi, I. X. (2022) *How to Raise an Anti-racist*, London, the Bodley Head.
A helpful guide to developing the next generation of anti-racists.

Kendi, I. X. (2023) *How to Be an Antiracist*, London, Vintage.
Explores personal and structural racism with accessible insight.

Malik, K. (2008) *Strange Fruit: Why Both Sides Are Wrong in the Race Debate*, London, Oneworld.
A nuanced and thought-provoking critique of race debates.

Neuberger, J. (2019) *Antisemitism: What It Is. What It Isn't. Why It Matters*, London, Weidenfeld & Nicolson.
A helpful review of anti-semitism.

Rutherford, A. (2021) *How to Argue with a Racist*, London, Weidenfeld & Nicolson.
Debunks pseudoscientific justifications for racism.

Shabi, R. (2024) *Off White: The Truth about Antisemitism*, London, Oneworld.
An interesting look at antisemitism as a form of racism.

West, K. (2025) *The Science of Racism: Everything You Need to Know but Probably Don't – Yet*, London, Bloomsbury.

Wilkerson, I. (2020) *Caste: The Origins of Our Discontents*, New York, Random House.

Books on colonialism, indigenous sovereignty and decolonization

Back, L. and Solomos, J. (eds) (2009) *Theories of Race and Racism,* 2nd edn, London, Routledge.
An academic reader exploring key theoretical developments.

Coulthard, G. (2014) *Red Skin, White Masks*, Minneapolis, MN, University of Minnesota Press.
Challenges liberal multicultural approaches to indigenous rights.

Jivraj, S. and Simpson, L. (eds) (2015) *Ethnic Identity and Inequalities in Britain*, Bristol, Policy Press.
Addresses changing dynamics of diversity.

Moreton-Robinson, A. (2015) *The White Possessive*, Minneapolis, MN, University of Minnesota Press.
An indigenous feminist critique of whiteness and land ownership.

Sanghera, S. (2021) *Empireland: How Imperialism Has Shaped Modern Britain*, London, Penguin.
An important overview of how colonialist and imperialist thinking persists to this day.

Simpson, L. (2011) *Dancing on Our Turtle's Back*, New York, Arbeiter Ring.
Advocates for indigenous resurgence rooted in culture and ceremony.

Smith, L. T. (2021) *Decolonizing Methodologies,* 3rd edn, London, Zed.
A foundational text in decolonial research theory and practice.

Sowemino, A. (2023) *Divided: Racism, Medicine and Why We Need to Decolonise Healthcare*, London, Profile Books.
A highly informative discussion of racism in healthcare.

Tuck, E. and Yang, K. W. (eds) (2014) *Youth Resistance Research and Theories of Change*, London, Routledge.
Features key scholarship including 'Decolonization is not a metaphor'.

Warsi, S. (2024) *Muslims Don't Matter*, London, The Bridge Street Press.
A telling critique of Islamophobia.

Williams, C. and Johnson, M. R. D. (2010) *Race and Ethnicity in a Welfare Society*, Maidenhead, Open University Press.
A critical look at race in welfare contexts.

Narrative and practice-based accounts

As a white person, I can offer an anti-racist perspective, but not a black one. It is therefore important for you to also read the accounts of people whose life is characterized by racism of one form or other.

Chehore, H. (ed.) (2021) *Social Work in the Face of Intersectional Racism: 'Still I Will Rise',* Independently published.
First-hand narratives of resilience and resistance.

Kivel, P. (2017) *Uprooting Racism: How White People Can Work for Racial Justice*, Gabriola Island, BC, New Society Publishers.
Practical guidance for white allies.

Moore, T., and Simango, G. (eds) *The Anti-racist Social Worker: Stories of Activism and Allied Health Professionals*, London, Routledge.
An insightful set of accounts.

Okeze-Tirado, V. (2023) *D.I.V.E.R.S.I.T.Y.: A Guide to Working with Diversity and Developing Cultural Sensitivity*, London, Jessica Kingsley Publishing.
A creative and experiential exploration of culturally sensitive practice.

Reid, W. and Maclean, S. (eds) (2021) *Outlanders: Hidden Narratives from Social Workers of Colour*, Birmingham, BASW.
Powerful narratives from practitioners across the Global Majority.

Sue, D. W. (2015) *Race Talk and the Conspiracy of Silence*, New York, Wiley.
Guidance for managing difficult dialogues on race.

Tedam, P. (2021) *Anti-Oppressive Social Work Practice*, London, Sage.
Offers frameworks with relevance beyond social work.

Academic journals

Engaging with peer-reviewed literature helps to stay informed about current debates, innovations and empirical research.

Decolonization and related matters
https://decolonization.org

Ethnic and Racial Studies
https://www.tandfonline.com/toc/rers20/current(https://www.tandfonline.com/toc/rers20/current)

International Indigenous Policy Journal
https://ojs.lib.uwo.ca/index.php/iipj

Journal of Indigenous Social Development
https://journalhosting.ucalgary.ca/index.php/jisd

Journal of Racial and Ethnic Health Disparities
https://www.springer.com/journal/40615(https://www.springer.com/
journal/40615)

Race, Ethnicity and Education
https://www.tandfonline.com/toc/cree20/current

Social Issues and Policy Review
https://spssi.onlinelibrary.wiley.com/journal/17512409(https://spssi.onlineli-
brary.wiley.com/journal/17512409)

Part three: Online resources, training and professional development

Websites and resource hubs

The Open University's OpenLearn facility has a wealth of resources at their Race and Ethnicity Hub: https://www.open.edu/openlearn/race-and-ethnicity-hub

Racial Equity Tools
https://www.racialequity.tools.org

Talking About Race – NMAAHC
https://nmaahc.si.edu/learn/talking-about-race

Center for the Study of Social Policy
https://cssp.org

First Nations Development Institute
https://www.firstnations.org

Aboriginal Healing Foundation (Canada) – Archive
http://www.ahf.ca

ACAS – Equality and Diversity
https://www.acas.org.uk

Black Lives Matter
https://blacklivesmatter.com

The Equality and Human Rights Commission
http://equalityhumanrights.com

Friends, Families and Travellers
https://www.gypsy-traveller.org

Hope Not Hate
https://www.hopenothate.org.uk

Human Rights Watch
https://www.hrw.org

Kick It Out
https://www.kickitout.org

The Runnymede Trust
https://www.runnymedetrust.org

World Jewish Congress – Combating Antisemitism
https://www.worldjewishcongress.org/en/focus-areas/combating-anti-
    semitism

References

Adibifar, K. and Monson, M. S. (2020) 'Workplace Subjective Alienation and Individuals' Well-being', *Journal of Economic Development, Environment and People*, 9(3), pp. 22–37, https://doi.org/10.26458/jedep.v9i3.669.

Aitchison, J. (2011) *The Articulate Mammal*, London, Routledge.

Alfred, T. and Corntassel, J. (2005) 'Being Indigenous: Resurgences against Contemporary Colonialism', *Government and Opposition,* 40(4), pp. 597–614.

Allen, D., Dove, D., Hulmes, A. and Moloney-Neachtain, M. (2021) 'Anti-racist Action in Practice: The Romani and Traveller Perspective', in Moore, T. and Simango, G. (eds) *The Anti-racist Social Worker: Stories of Activism by Social Care and Allied Health Professionals*, London, Routledge.

Ambedkar, B. R. (2014) *Annihilation of Caste: The Annotated Critical Edition*, London, Verso.

Avineri, N, Graham, L. R., Johnson, E. J., Riner, R. C. and Rosa, J. (2019) *Language and Social Justice in Practice*, London, Routledge.

Baddiel, D. (2021) *Jews Don't Count*, London, TLS Books.

Beauvoir, S. de (2011) *The Second Sex*, New York, Vintage.

Bordere, T. C. (2017) 'Disenfranchisement and Ambiguity in the Face of Loss: The Suffocated Grief of Sexual Assault Survivors', *Family Relations*, 66(1), pp. 29–45.

Byrne, L. (2024) *The Inequality of Wealth: Why It Matters and How to Fix It*, London, Head of Zeus.

Cavaliero, T. (2020) '"They're Trying to Teach Them What I Can Teach Them at Home, and Them Not a Traveller!": Introducing Irish Traveller Identity into the Curriculum', *Social Work and Social Sciences Review*, 22(1), pp. 83–102.

Chavez, L. J., Ornelas, I. J., Lyles, C. R. and Williams, E. C. (2015) Racial/Ethnic Workplace Discrimination', *American Journal of Preventive Medicine*, 48(1), pp. 42–9.

Cheng, E. and Agyepong, I. (2021) 'Contagion, Containment, and COVID-19: Anti-Asian Racism in the UK', *Journal of Ethnic and Migration Studies*, 47(2), pp. 456–72.

Chou, R. S. and Feagin, J. R. (2015) *The Myth of the Model Minority: Asian Americans Facing Racism,* 2nd edn, New York, Routledge.

Coeckelbergh, M. (2022) *The Political Philosophy of AI*, Cambridge, Polity.

Cohen, L. (2024) 'Diasporic Mysticism, Psychology, & Tarot: A Path to Decolonizing Intuitive Development', https://doi.org/10.31219/osf.io/wgp95_v1.

Corbally, J. (2009a) 'The Jarring Irish: Postwar Immigration to the Heart of Empire', *Radical History Review*, 2009(104), pp. 103–25.

Corbally, J. (2009b) *The Irish in Britain: Identity and Perception*, Dublin, Irish Academic Press.

Cox, G. R. (2022) *Sociology of Death and the American Indian*, London, Lexington Books.

Daniels, J. (2021) *White Supremacy and the Internet*, 2nd edn, Cambridge, Polity Press.

DiAngelo, R. (2019) *White Fragility: Why It's So Hard for White People to Talk about Racism*, London, Penguin.

Dijk, T. (2008) 'Discourse and the Denial of Racism', in *Discourse and Power*, Bloomsbury Academic, pp. 120–54. https://doi.org/10.1007/978-1-137-07299-3_6.

Doka, K. J. (1989) *Disenfranchised Grief Recognizing Hidden Sorrow*, San Francisco, CA, Jossey Bass.

Dorling, D. (2015) *Injustice: Why Social Inequality Still Persists*, 2nd edn, Bristol, Policy Press.

Dorling, D. (2018) *Peak Inequality: Britain's Ticking Time Bomb*, Bristol, Policy Press.

Eddo-Lodge, R. (2018) *Why I Am No Longer Talking to White People about Race*, London, Bloomsbury.

End the Virus of Racism (2021) *Anti-Asian Hate Crime Report 2020–2021*, London, End the Virus of Racism.

Fernando, S. (2018) *Institutional Racism in Psychiatry and Clinical Psychology: Race Matters in Mental Health*, London, Palgrave Macmillan.

Ferretti, F. (2017) 'Political Geographies, "Unfaithful" Translations and Anticolonialism: Ireland in Elisée Reclus's Geography and Biography', *Political Geography*, 59, pp. 11–23.

Foucault, M. (1980) *Power/Knowledge: Selected Interviews and Other Writings 1972-77*, ed. C. Gordon, Brighton, Harvester Press.

Frederickson, G. M. (2015) *Racism: A Short History*, Princeton, Princeton University Press.

Freire, P. (2000) *Pedagogy of the Oppressed*, London, Continuum.

Garner, S. (2007) *Whiteness: An Introduction*, London, Routledge.

Gervais, W. (2013) 'In Godlessness We Distrust: Using Social Psychology to Solve the Puzzle of Anti-atheist Prejudice', *Social and Personality Psychology Compass*, 7(6), pp. 366–77.

Gervais, W., Shariff, A. and Norenzayan, A. (2011) 'Do You Believe in Atheists? Distrust Is Central to Anti-atheist Prejudice', *Journal of Personality and Social Psychology*, 101(6), pp. 1189–206.

Glenn, E. N. (2008) 'Yearning for Lightness: Transnational Circuits in the Marketing and Consumption of Skin Lighteners', *Gender & Society*, 22(3), pp. 281–302.

Gramsci, A. (1998) *Selections from the Prison Notebooks*, London, Lawrence & Wishart.

Greenslade, R. (2004) *Press Gang: How Newspapers Make Profits from Propaganda*, London, Macmillan.

Griffiths, J. (2021) *Speak Not: Empire, Identity and the Politics of Language*, London, Zed.

Hariri, Y., Magdy, W. and Wolters, M. (2019) 'Arabs and Atheism: Religious Discussions in the Arab Twittersphere', in Weber, I., et al. (ed.) *Social Informatics. SocInfo 2019. Lecture Notes in Computer Science*, vol. 11864, Cham, Springer, https://doi.org/10.1007/978-3-030-34971-4_2.

Hart, V. (2021) '"If Not Now, When?" On Jewishness and Challenging Anti-semitism', in Moore, T. and Simango, G. (eds) *The Anti-racist Social Worker: Stories of Activism by Social Care and Allied Health Professionals*, London, Routledge.

Hechter, M. (1999) *Internal Colonialism: The Celtic Fringe in British National Development, 1536–1966*, New Brunswick, NJ, Transaction Publishers.

Hernon, I. (2020) *Anti-semitism and the Left*, Stroud, Amberley.

Hickman, M., Crowley, H. and Mai, N. (2005) *'Above Us the Sky': Representations of Irishness in Britain*, London, London Metropolitan University.

Hickman, M. and Walter, B. (1997) *Discrimination and the Irish Community in Britain: A Report for the Commission for Racial Equality*, London, Commission for Racial Equality.

Hout, M. and Connor, S. (2008) 'The Normalisation of Substance Abuse among Young Travellers in Ireland', *Journal of Ethnicity in Substance Abuse*, 7(1), pp. 5–21.

Howard, L. (2021) 'Becoming an Anti-racist Ally', in Moore, T. and Simango, G. (eds) *The Anti-racist Social Worker: Stories of Activism by Social Care and Allied Health Professionals*, London, Routledge.

Hunter, M. (2005) *Race, Gender and the Politics of Skin Tone,* New York, Routledge.

Hunter, M. (2007) 'The Persistent Problem of Colorism: Skin Tone, Status, and Inequality', *Sociology Compass*, 1(1), pp. 237–54.

Huq, R. A. (2015) *The Psychology of Employee Empowerment: Concepts, Critical Themes and a Framework for Implementation*, Farnham, Gower.

Huws, C. Ff. (2018) 'Why Racism against Welsh People Is Still Racism', *The Conversation*, https://theconversation.com/why-racism-against-welsh-people-is-still-racism-96303.

Ison, R. and Straw, E. (2020) *The Hidden Power of Systems Thinking: Governance in a Climate Emergency*, London, Routledge.

Jaeggi, R. (2016) *Alienation*, New York, Columbia University Press.

Jaffe, S. (2021) *Work Won't Love You Back: How Devotion to Our Jobs Keeps Us Exploited, Exhausted and Alone*, London, Hurst & Company.

Katoto, D. and Mohamed, O. (2021) 'Exploring Anti-racism in Social Work Education', in Reid, W. and Maclean, S. (eds) *Outlanders: Hidden Narratives from Social Workers of Colour from Black & Other Global Majority Communities*, Birmingham, BASW.

Khan, O. (2022) *Racism and COVID-19: Racial Disparities and the Pandemic in the UK*, London, Runnymede Trust.

Khanna, V. (2024) 'Roma Vulnerability before the European Court of Human Rights: Towards a Structural Account', *Netherlands Quarterly of Human Rights*, 42(4), pp. 340–62.

Kim, J., Ju, G., Lee, S., Shin, C., Son, J., Kim, S. ... and Chung, S. (2023) 'The Relationship Between Anger and Suicidality', *Mood and Emotion*, 21(3), pp. 86–94.

Kotýnková, M. (2020) 'Economic Migration of Eastern Europeans in the UK after the UK Referendum Held in 2016', in *The 19th International Scientific Conference Globalization and Its Socio-Economic Consequences 2019 – Sustainability in the Global-Knowledge Economy*, SHS Web of Conferences, vol. 74, https://doi.org/10.1051/shsconf/20207405011.

Lammy, D. (2017) *The Lammy Review: An Independent Review into the Treatment of, and Outcomes for Black, Asian and Minority Ethnic Individuals in the Criminal Justice System*, London, HMSO.

Li, E. P., Min, H. J., Belk, R. W., Kimura, J. and Bahl, S. (2008) 'Skin Lightening and Beauty in Four Asian Cultures', *Advances in Consumer Research*, 35, pp. 444–9.

Lindquist, S. (2007) *Terra Nullius: A Journey Through No One's Land*, New York, the New Press.

Livings, M. S., Smith-Greenaway, E., Margolis, R. and Verdery, A. M. (2022) 'Bereavement & Mental Health: The Generational Consequences of a Grandparent's Death', *SSM – Mental Health*, 2, https://doi.org/10.1016/j.ssmmh.2022.100100.

Lorde, A. (1988) *A Burst of Light: And Other Essay*, Ithaca, NY, Firebrand Books.

Loveland, M. T. and Popescu, D. (2016) 'The Gypsy Threat Narrative', *Humanity & Society*, 40(3), pp. 329–52.

Lulle, A., Moroşanu, L. and King, R. (2017) 'And Then Came Brexit: Experiences and Future Plans of Young EU Migrants in the London Region', *Population Space and Place*, 24(1), p. e2122, https://doi.org/10.1002/psp.2122.

MacRaild, D. M. (1999) *Irish Migrants in Modern Britain, 1750–1922*, London, Macmillan.

Madden, H., Harris, J., Blickem, C., Harrison, R. and Timpson, H. (2017) '"Always Paracetamol, They Give Them Paracetamol for Everything": A Qualitative Study Examining Eastern European Migrants' Experiences of the UK Health Service', *BMC Health Services Research*, 17(1), p. 604, https://doi.org/10.1186/s12913-017-2526-3.

Malik, K. (2008) *Strange Fruit: Why Both Sides are Wrong in the Race Debate*, Oxford, One World.

Mama, A. (1989) *The Hidden Struggle*, London, LRHRU/Runnymede Trust.

Marcus, G. (2019) *Gypsy and Traveller Girls; Silence, Agency and Power*, London, Palgrave Macmillan.

May, V. M. (2015) *Pursuing Intersectionality: Unsettling Dominant Imaginaries*, London, Routledge.

McGinnity, F. and Lunn, P. (2011) 'Measuring Discrimination Facing Ethnic Minority Job Applicants: An Irish Experiment', *Work Employment and Society*, 25(4), pp. 693–708.

McGinnity, F., Quinn, E., McCullough, E., Enright, S. and Curristan, S. (2021) *Measures to Combat Racial Discrimination and Promote Diversity in the Labour Market: A Review of Evidence*, ESRI Survey and Statistical Report Series 110, Dublin, ESRI.

McNeil-Young, V., Mosley, D., Bellamy, P., Lewis, A. and Hernandez, C. (2023) 'Storying Survival: An Approach to Radical Healing for the Black Community', *Journal of Counseling Psychology*, 70(3), pp. 276–92.

Mekawi, Y. and Todd, N. R. (2021) 'Focusing the Lens to See More Clearly: Overcoming Definitional Challenges and Identifying New Directions in Racial Microaggressions Research', *Perspectives on Psychological Science*, 16(5), pp. 972–90.

Mishra, V. (2015) 'Fair & Lovely and the Construction of the Contemporary Indian Woman', *Social Semiotics*, 25(3), pp. 278–92.

Monbiot, G. and Hutchinson, P. (2024) *The Invisible Doctrine: The Secret History of Neoliberalism (& How It Came to Control Your Life)*, London, Penguin.

Monk, E. P. (2014) 'Skin Tone Stratification among Black Americans, 2001–2003', *Social Forces*, 92(4), pp. 1313–17.

Montefiore, S. S. (2021) *The World: A Family Holiday*, London, Weidenfeld and Nicolson.

Moreira, T., Martins, J., Silva, C., Luna, E. B., Martins, J., Moreira, D. A. … and Rosário, P. (2023) 'Building Partnerships in Education through a Story-tool Based Intervention:

Parental Involvement Experiences among Families with Roma Backgrounds', *Frontiers in Psychology*, 14, p. 1012568, https://doi.org/10.3389/fpsyg.2023.1012568.

Moreton-Robinson, A. (2015) *The White Possessive: Property, Power, and Indigenous Sovereignty*, Indianapolis, MN, University of Minnesota Press.

Naidoo, R. (2020) 'Branding Colourism: The Fair & Lovely Controversy and the Ethics of Rebranding', *Media Watch*, 11(3), pp. 565–73.

Nelson, J., Dunn, K. and Paradies, Y. (2011) 'Bystander Anti-racism: A Review of the Literature', *Analyses of Social Issues and Public Policy*, 11(1), pp. 263–84.

Neuberger, J. (2019) *Antisemitism: What It Is. What It Isn't. Why It Matters*, London, Weidenfeld and Nicolson.

Ng, E. S., Chung, A. M. and Yeung, K. (2021) 'From Exotic to Threatening: A Review of Anti-Asian Racism in Western Societies', *Race, Ethnicity and Education*, 24(3), pp. 319–36.

Obama, B. (2020) *A Promised Land*, London, Viking.

Olusoga, D. (2016) *Black and British: A Forgotten History*, London, Macmillan.

Parameswaran, R. and Cardoza, K. (2009) 'Melanin on the Margins: Advertising and the Cultural Politics of Fair/Light/White Beauty in India', *Journalism & Communication Monographs*, 11(3), pp. 213–74.

Penketh, L. (2000) *Tackling Institutional Racism*, Bristol, Policy Press.

Phung, V., Asghar, Z., Matiti, M. and Siriwardena, A. (2020) 'Understanding How Eastern European Migrants Use and Experience UK Health Services: A Systematic Scoping Review', *BMC Health Services Research*, 20(1), p. 173, https://doi.org/10.1186/s12913-020-4987-z.

Public Health England (2020) *Beyond the Data: Understanding the Impact of COVID-19 on BAME Groups*, London, PHE.

Rosenblatt, P. (2016) 'Cultural Competence and Humility', in Harris, D. L. and Bordere, T. C. (eds) *Handbook of Social Justice in Loss and Grief: Exploring Diversity, Equity, and Exclusion*, New York, Routledge..

Rosino, M. and Hughey, M. (2016) 'Speaking through Silence: Racial Discourse and Identity Construction in Mass-mediated Debates on the 'War on Drugs'', *Social Currents*, 4(3), pp. 246–64.

Rutherford, A. (2021) *How to Argue with a Racist: History, Science, Race and Reality*, London, Weidenfeld & Nicolson.

Ryan, W. (1971) *Blaming the Victim*, New York, Pantheon.

Rzepnikowska, A. (2018) 'Racism and Xenophobia Experienced by Polish Migrants in the UK Before and After Brexit Vote', *Journal of Ethnic and Migration Studies*, 45(1), pp. 61–77.

Sabharwal, N. S. and Sonalkar, W. (2015). 'Dalit Women in India: At the Crossroads of Gender, Class, and Caste', *Global Justice*, 8(1).

Said, E. W. (1978) *Orientalism*, New York, Pantheon Books.

Salter, P. S. and Adams, G. (2016) 'On the Intentionality of Cultural Products: Representations of Black History as Psychological Affordances', *Frontiers in Psychology*, 7, p. 1166, https://doi.org/10.3389/fpsyg.2016.01166.

Sanghera, S. (2021) *Empireland: How Imperialism Has Shaped Modern Britain*, London, Penguin.

Sarafian, I., Robinson, A., Christov, A. and Tarchini, A. (2024) 'In the Margins of Stigma: Health Inequalities among Bulgarian Roma in a Post-covid-19 UK', *BMJ Global Health*, 9(11), https://doi.org/10.1136/bmjgh-2024-015686.

Sartre, J.-P. (1973) *Search for a Method*, New York, Vintage.

Sartre, J.-P. (2020) *Being and Nothingness: An Essay in Phenomenological Ontology*, London, Routledge.

Shabi, R. (2024) *Off-white: The Truth about Antisemitism*, London, Oneworld.

Shaver, J., Sibley, C., Osborne, D. and Bulbulia, J. (2017) 'News Exposure Predicts Anti-Muslim Prejudice', *PLOS One*, 12(3), p. e0174606, https://doi.org/10.1371/journal.pone.0174606.

Shavit, A. (2014) *My Promised Land: The Triumph and Tragedy of Israel*, London, Scribe Publications.

Shucksmith, M. (2012) 'Class, Power and Inequality in Rural Areas: Beyond Social Exclusion?' *Sociologia Ruralis*, 52(4), pp. 377–97.

Skelton, G. (2017) 'Reclaiming and Embracing Spirituality as a Legitimate Facet of Education', in Bhatti-Sinclair, K. and Smethurst, C. (eds) *Diversity, Difference and Dilemmas; Analysing Concepts and Developing Skills*, Maidenhead, Open University Press.

Sowemimo, A. (2023) *Divided: Racism. Medicine and Why We Need to Decolonise Healthcare*, London, Profile Books.

Tereshchenko, A., Bradbury, A. and Archer, L. (2019) 'Eastern European Migrants' Experiences of Racism in English Schools: Positions of Marginal Whiteness and Linguistic Otherness', *Whiteness and Education*, 4(1), pp. 53–71.

Thomas, W. I. and Thomas, D. S. (1923) *The Child in America: Behaviour Problems and Programs,* New York, Alfred A. Knopf.

Thomas-Jackson, S. C., Sharp, E. A., Bordere, T. C. and Moonshower, M. (2025) 'Disrupting Neoliberalism in the Academy: Normalizing Loss and Enfranchising Student Grief', *Journal of Family Theory & Review*, 17(1), pp. 92–111.

Thompson, N. (2007) *Power and Empowerment*, Lyme Regis, Russell House Publishing.

Thompson, N. (2017a) *Social Problems and Social Justice*, London, Bloomsbury.

Thompson, N. (2017b) *Theorizing Practice*, 2nd edn, London, Bloomsbury.

Thompson, N. (2018a) *Applied Sociology*, New York, Routledge.

Thompson, N. (2018b) *Effective Communication*, 3rd edn, London, Bloomsbury.

Thompson, N. (2018c) *Promoting Equality: Working with Diversity and Difference*, 4th edn, London, Bloomsbury.

Thompson, N. (2019) *Mental Health and Well-being: Alternatives to the Medical Model*, New York, Routledge.

Thompson, N. (2021) *Anti-discriminatory Practice: Equality, Diversity and Social Justice*, 7th edn, London, Bloomsbury.

Thompson, N. (2024) *Managing Stress*, 2nd edn, London, Routledge.

Thompson, N. (2025) *Authentic Leadership Revisited*, 2nd edn, Cheltenham, Edward Elgar Publishing.

Thompson, N. and Moss, B. (2026a) *Values-based Practice*, 2nd edn, London, Routledge.

Thompson, N. and Moss, B. (2026b) *Spirituality and Religion*, 2nd edn, London, Routledge.

Thompson, S. and Thompson, N. (2023) *The Critically Reflective Practitioner*, 3rd edn, London, Bloomsbury.

Thompson, S., Woods, J. and Katzenellenbogen, J. (2012) 'The Quality of Indigenous Identification in Administrative Health Data in Australia: Insights from Studies Using Data Linkage', *BMC Medical Informatics and Decision Making*, 12(1), p. 133, https://doi.org/10.1186/1472-6947-12-133.

Thorat, S. and Newman, K. S. (2010) *Blocked by Caste: Economic Discrimination in Modern India,* New Delhi, Oxford University Press.

Thurber, K., Thandrayen, J., Maddox, R., Barrett, E., Walker, J., Priest, N. ... and Lovett, R. (2021) 'Reflection on Modern Methods: Statistical, Policy and Ethical Implications of Using Age-standardized Health Indicators to Quantify Inequities', *International Journal of Epidemiology*, 51(1), pp. 324–33.

Tilki, M., Ryan, L., D'Angelo, A. and Sales, R. (2009) *The Forgotten Irish: A Research Report for the Irish Chaplaincy in Britain*, London, Irish Chaplaincy in Britain.

Treuer, D. (2019) *The Heartbeat of Wounded Knee: Native Americans from 1890 to the Present,* London, Corsair.

Truth and Reconciliation Commission of Canada (2015) *Honouring the Truth, Reconciling for the Future: Summary of the Final Report of the Truth and Reconciliation Commission of Canada.*

United Nations (2007) *United Nations Declaration on the Rights of Indigenous Peoples.*

Walker, A. (1982) *In Search of Our Mothers' Gardens: Womanist Prose.* San Diego, Harcourt Brace Jovanovich.

Warsi, S. (2024) *Muslims Don't Matter*, London, The Bridge Street Press.

West, K. (2025) *The Science of Racism: Everything You Need to Know but Probably Don't – Yet,* London, Picador.

Wilkerson, I. (2020) *Caste: The Origins of Our Discontents*, New York, Random House.

Wilkinson, R. and Pickett, K. (2011) *The Spirit Level: Why More Equal Societies almost Always Do Better*, London, Penguin.

Wilkinson, R. and Pickett, K. (2018) *The Inner Level: How More Equal Societies Reduce Stress, Restore Sanity and Improve Everyone's Well-being,* London, Allen Lane.

Williams, E. (2022) *Capitalism and Slavery*, London, Penguin.

Witgen, M. J. (2022) *Seeing Red: Indigenous Land, American Expansion and the Political Economy of Plunder in North America*, Williamsburg, VA, Omohundro Institute of Early American History and Culture; and Chapel Hill, NC, University of North Carolina Press.

Wood, K. M. and McMahon, H. G. (2024) 'Supporting Students Who Are Grieving: Interventions and Practices for School Counselors'. *Professional School Counselling*, 28(1b). https://doi.org/10.1177/2156759x241247163.

Yeh, D. (2014) *Becoming British Chinese: Culture, Identity and Ethnicity in the Diaspora*, Basingstoke, Palgrave Macmillan.

Yengde, S. (2018) *Caste Matters*, Gurgaon, India, Penguin Random House.

Zwick-Maitreyi, M., Soundararajan, T., Dar, N., Bheel, R.F. and Balakrishnan, P. (2018) *Caste in the United States: A Survey of Caste among South Asian Americans*, Oakland, CA: Equality Labs.

Zwysen, W., Stasio, V. D. and Heath, A. (2020) 'Ethnic Penalties and Hiring Discrimination: Comparing Results from Observational Studies with Field Experiments in the UK', *Sociology*, 55(2), pp. 263–82.

For Product Safety Concerns and Information please contact our EU
representative GPSR@taylorandfrancis.com
Taylor & Francis Verlag GmbH, Kaufingerstraße 24, 80331 München, Germany

www.ingramcontent.com/pod-product-compliance
Lightning Source LLC
Chambersburg PA
CBHW052009270326
41929CB00015B/2844

*9 7 8 1 0 4 1 1 3 1 2 3 6 *